*Enriching Your Faith and Prayer Life
Through the Many Names of Jesus*

Christ the Merciful

Brother Victor-Antoine d'Avila-Latourrette

PARACLETE PRESS
BREWSTER, MASSACHUSETTS

2016 First Printing

Christ the Merciful: Enriching Your Faith and Prayer Life Through the Many Names of Jesus

Copyright © 2016 by Brother Victor-Antoine d'Avila-Latourrette

ISBN 978-1-61261-772-5

Unless otherwise indicated, Scripture texts are taken from the New Revised Standard Version Bible, copyright 1989, Division of Christian Education of the National Council of the Churches of Christ in the United States of America. Used by permission. All rights reserved.

Scripture texts marked ESV (The Holy Bible, English Standard Version ®) copyright © 2001 by Crossway, a publishing ministry of Good News Publishers. ESV® Text Edition: 2011. The ESV® text has been reproduced in cooperation with and by permission of the Good News Publishers. Unauthorized reproduction of this publication is prohibited. All rights reserved.

Scripture texts marked with DRA are taken from the Douay-Rheims 1899 American Edition, which is in the public domain.

Scripture texts in this work marked NABRE are taken from the *New American Bible, revised edition* © 2010, 1991, 1986, 1970 Confraternity of Christian Doctrine, Washington, DC, and are used by permission of the copyright owner. All Rights Reserved. No part of the New American Bible may be reproduced in any form without permission in writing from the copyright owner.

Scripture texts marked NASB are taken from the New American Standard Bible, copyright © 1960, 1962, 1963, 1968, 1971, 1972, 1973, 1975, 1977, 1995 by The Lockman Foundation. Used by permission.

Scripture quotations marked NIV are taken from THE HOLY BIBLE, NEW INTERNATIONAL VERSION © NIV © Copyright © 1973, 1978, 1984 by International Bible Society ®. Used by permission. All rights reserved worldwide.

Scripture texts marked RSV are from the Revised Standard Version, Second Edition, 1971 copyright by the National Council of the Churches of Christ of the United States of America, Division of Christian Education, and published in The New Oxford Annotated Expanded Edition, 1977.

Excerpts marked LM are taken from the *Lectionary for Mass for Use in the Dioceses of the United States of America, second typical edition* © 2001, 1998, 1997, 1986, 1970 Confraternity of Christian Doctrine, Inc., Washington, DC. Used with permission. All rights reserved. No portion of this text may be reproduced by any means without permission in writing from the copyright owner.

Prayers taken from *The Syriac Fathers on Prayer and the Spiritual Life,* introduced and translated by Sebastian Brock. Copyright 1987 by Cistercian Publications, Inc. © 2008 by Order of Saint Benedict, Collegeville, Minnesota. Used with permission.

The Paraclete Press name and logo (dove on cross) are trademarks of Paraclete Press, Inc.

Library of Congress Cataloging-in-Publication Data

<blockquote>

Names: D'Avila-Latourrette, Victor-Antoine, author.

Title: Christ the merciful : enriching your faith and prayer life through the many names of Jesus / Brother Victor-Antoine D'Avila-Latourrette.

Description: Brewster MA : Paraclete Press Inc., 2016. | Includes bibliographical references.

Identifiers: LCCN 2016040546 | ISBN 9781612617725 (trade paper)

Subjects: LCSH: Jesus Christ--Name. | Spiritual life--Christianity.

Classification: LCC BT590.N2 D38 2016 | DDC 232--dc23

LC record available at https://lccn.loc.gov/2016040546

</blockquote>

10 9 8 7 6 5 4 3 2 1

Published by Paraclete Press
Brewster, Massachusetts
www.paracletepress.com
Printed in the United States of America

CONTENTS

To Christ the Merciful One:
to the Sacred Heart of our Lord Jesus Christ, our Lord and
  savior,
to the eternal Light from the Father and his eternal delight,
fountain of divine mercy and temple of the Holy Spirit,
clothed in his wisdom and holiness,
incarnate, made human in a Virgin Mother's womb,
by John the Baptist heralded,
adopted and trained by noble Joseph the humble carpenter
  of Nazareth,
by Kings, Prophets, and Patriarchs, announced from the
  beginning of the ages
and source of unparalleled and impressible joy for all the
  angels and saints,
I totally trust in you, and commend myself to your gentle
  mercy,
which alone endures forever.

And in loving memory of Dorothy Day,
an inspiration during our earthly pilgrimage,
and to David Boatwright,
a loyal friend in all life's seasons
and a faithful follower of Christ the Merciful,
continuing the works of mercy
as taught to us in the Gospels.

—Brother Victor-Antoine d'Avila-Latourrette

FOREWORD

Thomas Merton was once asked, "How do you pray?" His response was startlingly simple: "How I pray is—I breathe." Breathe, breathing, in-spiring. Breathing has been described as the oldest therapy known to man. Deeper breathing brings immediate calm. It is central to yogic practice (pranayama), and it is also part of the Eastern Orthodox contemplative practice of hesychasm and many other spiritual disciplines. It is fundamental in a variety of Buddhist meditative practices—from vipassana to Zen. Thich Nhat Hanh has described his teaching as simply guiding people to breathe mindfully.

The essence of the Christian path is transformation in Christ. In fact, all genuine spirituality is about transformation. Our tradition often quotes in this context Saint Paul's phrase in 2 Corinthians 3:18 that we are "transformed from glory to glory"—from image to greater image—by the Spirit who is creative breath.

At Creation the Spirit, the divine breath, gave us the first gift; Christ's spirit re-creates us, the second gift. The Irish theologian John Scotus Eriugena (815–877) distinguishes between the *datum* (the already given) and the *donum* (the gift): creation and new creation. Saint Paul in 1 Corinthians

15 talks about who we are in Adam and who we continue to become in Christ. In Adam we became living beings. In Christ we become life-giving spirit, generative, overflowing with gifts of the Spirit.

Brother Victor's book was finished as his health was severely compromised. It is a testament to perseverance and commitment. There are really two themes intertwined in his meditation: the Spirit as breath and God's loving mercy. His work frequently quotes texts from Eastern fathers and Eastern liturgy—and thus is witness to his ongoing integration of Christian West and Christian East. It follows the advice of Saint John Paul II that we must increasingly breathe from both lungs—East and West.

As we breathe in the Spirit of God, may mercy and compassion flow over to all creation.

Sister Donald Corcoran, OSB
Feast of Saint Francis, 2015

INTRODUCTION

In our prayer lives, it can be easy to settle on one fixed image of Christ. Perhaps we think of a statue or icon from our local church, or a painting or illustration we keep at home. While such a constant reference point can be a useful gateway to prayer, it can also limit our conception of all that Christ is, was, and can be. Similarly, if we do not acknowledge Christ's many names and symbolic identities—from traditional titles such as "Lord" and "Lamb of God" to more mystical designations such as the "Keeper of the Gate"—we lose the opportunity to meet him in his rich complexity and deepen our relationship with him.

When we meditate on his names, Christ inspires us to revise our expectations of him. He invites us to move beyond our self-centered ideas of who we think he *should* be and focus instead on his ever-changing, ever-renewed presence in our lives. This may move us spiritually and emotionally, and it may present us with a newfound understanding of his grace. It also may force us to encounter him in ways we never imagined or thought possible. Having an array of his names to call upon, we know we can embrace such moments with confidence, growing in knowledge and love.

To pray with and in Christ means attempting to transcend our limited, sometimes doctrinal or parochial, understandings of who he is. Rather than assigning him an identity we are comfortable with, we must allow ourselves to be challenged by the many dimensions of his human personality and divine nature. It may not be easy to open ourselves to the great mystery contained within his images, titles, and symbols, but to do so is to begin to partake of the abundance of his life and the life he imparts to us.

In all of this, we must remember that Christ's mystery is so rich that it can encompass all strands of tradition—the biblical, the monastic, and the patristic—as well as anything our imaginations can conceive. We should always be open to new designations for Christ and prepared to gather them into our prayer. This is the work of the contemplative, to unite Christ's many names into a harmonious whole. It is the reason why the early monks liked to pray the name of Jesus, for it evoked his different titles yet blended them into the singular mystery of the eternal Word.

We work through a variety of names of Christ to get a glimpse into the unified whole. These titles may be best understood in context, through liturgical action, *lectio divina*, and private prayer. To refer to Christ as the "Bread of Life," for instance, makes the most sense when we partake of the tangible Eucharist. Each of us is called to discover the particular richness of each title, though individuals may prefer one title or another. This individual attraction depends on the operation of the Holy Spirit in the soul of the believer.

The designations presented here are like lampposts on the road to eternity, guiding us, pointing us always toward Christ's transcendent mystery. It is up to us to assimilate this mystery in the light of the Holy Spirit, who alone can reveal the depths of Christ's presence. These titles may help us along the way, showing us in their singularity something of the great unification at the end of the ages—when, in the words of Saint Paul, Christ will finally be "all in all."

PART I

CHRIST
in Images, Names, and Symbols

1.

We Confess Christ, Our God

Let the same mind be in you that was in Christ Jesus, who, though he was in the form of God, did not regard equality with God as something to be exploited, but emptied himself, taking the form of a slave, being born in human likeness. And being found in human form, he humbled himself and became obedient to the point of death—even death on a cross. Therefore God also highly exalted him and gave him the name that is above every name, so that at the name of Jesus every knee should bend, in heaven and on earth and under the earth, and every tongue should confess that Jesus Christ is Lord, to the glory of God the Father.
—Philippians 2:5–11

We confess Jesus Christ to be a Man like us, a Man without vice, and, meanwhile, a perfect God, who with the Holy Spirit is of the same essence with the Father—who is indivisible as one God of the Holy Trinity, in unbreakable Three Persons, as an indivisible nature of glory.
—Saint Gregory of Narek,
Doctor of the Universal Church

I am often reminded of an attitude that makes the monastic witness somehow unique in our present times. It is the clear and undisputed confession on the part of the monk that Christ alone is true God and true man. From the times of the apostles to the era of the martyrs, Christ's followers paid the ultimate price with their life and blood for the privilege of confessing Christ. Their confession of Christ as true God and true man was more than just paying lip service to a doctrine. They went beyond that, beyond a routine profession of faith such as the one we make every Sunday when we recite the Nicene Creed, beautiful as this may be. Confessing Christ as God was very personal to them. It meant being ready to give one's life.

After the persecution of Christians came to an end during the reign of Constantine, thus ceasing the witness of the martyrs, the Holy Spirit prompted a group of fervent followers of Christ to find a new way of confessing him in a faithful way. The Spirit of God inspired these Christians to withdraw to the harsh solitude of the desert, be it of Egypt or Palestine, and from there testify through the humble witness of their lives to Christ's unique truth, that he alone is both God and man. How were they able to accomplish this type of witnessing? By continual prayer, humble repentance, and asceticism, an asceticism that implied complete fidelity to the teachings of the Gospel. Living the totality of the Gospel teachings in an authentic manner, daily, all of them without exception expressed a new way of confessing Christ to both Christians and pagans alike. The monastic movement had as its humble origin only one purpose: the continuation of daily confessing Christ to the world, the dark pagan world of that particular time, not unlike our own.

For the early Christians, the martyrs and first monastics, this daily confessing of Christ meant attesting to the unique reality of him who came down from heaven, from the Father's bosom, who was God and also man. In the Gospels there were different titles to describe the Lord. "Son of God" and "Son of Man" are two among many more. The title "Son of God" speaks directly to Jesus's divine origins, while "Son of Man" makes clear that he is also one of us—indeed, a true representative of humankind.

Confessing Christ, both in the early centuries and now, means simply proclaiming, firmly and without ambiguity, that Christ is the Son of God. He is one with his heavenly Father, sharing from all eternity the same divine nature; and at the same time, he is one with us, sharing our human nature, which he received from his conception by a virgin mother.

The confession of Christ the God-man encompasses all these expressions: proclamation, affirmation, and testimony that the Son of God, in his love for mankind, in his eternal and divine form, assumed the humbleness and lowliness of our human nature. In doing so, he became the living, and only, bridge between divinity and humanity. As Saint Paul says, "Blessed be the God and Father of our Lord Jesus Christ, who has blessed us in Christ with every spiritual blessing in the heavenly places, just as he chose us in Christ before the foundation of the world to be holy and blameless before him in love. He destined us for adoption as his children, through Jesus Christ, according to the good plea-sure of his will, to the praise of his glorious grace that he freely bestowed on us in the Beloved" (Eph. 1:3–6).

Saint Cyril of Alexandria, a remarkable church father, explained in exact words what this confession implied in the development of early apostolic doctrine. In his treatise *Against Those Who Are Unwilling to Confess that the Holy Virgin Is Theotokos*, he writes, "Christ is confessed as God and man conjointly. But this is not how the apostles preached to us the divine Gospel. On the contrary, they have handed down to us one Christ, who is both God and man. The apostle John proclaims in his Gospel, 'In the beginning was the Word, and the Word was with God, and the Word was God,' and then he adds, 'And the Word was made flesh and dwelt among us.' The divinely inspired scriptures attri-bute to him conjointly the things which belong by nature to the divinity and those things which belong to the nature of man. In this, the economy of the union is clearly seen."[2]

> *The fact that God became a human being*
> *is a firm confirmation of our hope*
> *for the divine transformation of human nature.*
> *Humanity will be made divine*
> *just as God himself became a man.*
> *He who became man without any sin*
> *will deify human nature,*
> *yet without changing it into divine nature,*
> *and he will personally exalt it as high*
> *as he was once brought low for humanity's sake.*

This is the mystical teaching
of the great apostle Paul, who said:
"In the age to come he will make manifest
the overflowing riches of his grace."
—Saint Maximus the Confessor

2.

In the Father's Bosom:
The Eternal Word

*I will tell you of the decree of the LORD: He said to me,
"You are my son; today I have begotten you."*
—Psalm 2:7

*In the beginning was the Word, and the Word was with
God, and the Word was God. He was in the beginning
with God. All things came into being through him, and
without him not one thing came into being. What has
come into being in him was life, and the life was the
light of all the people. The light shines in the darkness,
and the darkness did not overcome it. . . . And the Word
became flesh and lived among us, and we have seen his
glory, the glory as of a father's only son, full of grace and
truth. . . . No one has ever seen God. It is God the only
Son, who is close to the Father's heart, who has made
him known.*
—John 1:1–5, 14, 18

Yours is princely power in the day of your birth, in holy splendor; before the daystar, like the dew, I have begotten you.

—Psalm 110:3 (LM)

In the prologue of the Gospel of John, we learn distinctly that the Logos, the Word, the second person of the Holy Trinity, existed from all eternity, and that he is coequal to the Father. In the Old Testament, the Lord revealed himself as the one eternal God, and he stopped there for the time being. Then, in the "fullness of time," according to Saint Paul, Christ became flesh like us to reveal the eternal reality that God coexists in three divine persons: the Father, the Son-Word, and the Spirit. The three are coequal and share in the one God's essence and being, and they coexist together in a permanent communion of love. God is one, and his oneness is manifested in the unique, perfect, loving interaction of the three divine persons with each other. As an early church father used to explain: "The Father reposes in the Son, and the Son reposes in the Father, and the Spirit reposes in the Father and the Son."

Long before the Word's arrival into our world, Psalm 2 already alludes to the divine sonship, communicating God's ever-ancient truth. The Father says to the Word: "*You are my Son, today I have begotten you.*" Yes, long before the creation of the world, in holy splendor, in the actual "today" of eternity—the "endless day" without beginning or end— the Father begets the Son. In that ongoing eternal day, the ever-existing Father gives birth to an ever-existing Son, the

Father's own spoken Word. The Word, the Logos, God's Son is in all things equal to his Father: God from God, Light from Light, true God from true God. In the words of the Epistle to the Hebrews, "the reflection of God's glory and the exact imprint of God's very being, he sustains all things by his powerful word" (Heb. 1:3).

The small hints communicated to us in the Sacred Scriptures, particularly in the Gospels, tell us that God is life itself. He is the source of all life. His infinite fruitfulness expands to such an extent that, in his eternal counsel, he decides to send the Word into the world so that, one day, humankind can participate fully in that all-fruitful, eternal, divine life. God so loved the world, says the apostle John, that he sent his only Son, the eternal Word, so that everyone who believes in him may not perish, but may have eternal life. "Indeed, God did not send the Son into the world to condemn the world, but in order that the world might be saved through him" (John 3:16–17).

Saint Athanasius of Alexandria, one of the remarkable early church fathers, affirms that the Son, the Word, the Logos, is born before the ages. He explains that "before the ages" means "non-temporal," totally outside time or before time existed. This means the Word proceeded from the Father before the ages or time itself. He goes further to say that this being born from the Father is more a condition and not an act or an event. To say that Christ, the Word of God, is born from the Father in God's "eternal now" means simply that Christ is born from the Father without an actual birth; that is, he was and existed as long as the Father was and existed. Ultimately we acknowledge that the Word has always existed in the Father's bosom, *"in sinu Patris,"* in eternity, outside time or events enacted within time.

Later on, after the mystery of the Incarnation is accomplished, the Gospels record two instances where the Father testifies that Christ is the Son of God. These two glorious moments are Christ's Theophany in the Jordan and his Transfiguration on Mount Tabor, when the Father's voice is clearly heard, saying, "This is my beloved Son, in whom I am well pleased." As the beautiful Troparion we sing during the Theophany feast remarks, the Holy Spirit's descending as a dove over Christ's head at the moment of his baptism in the Jordan "confirms the truth of the Father's words."

All day, all night, my soul is taken up with you, O Lord,
  and I seek you.
Your Holy Spirit draws me to seek you,
and the remembrance of you makes my mind glad.
My soul came to love you,
and rejoices that you are my God and my Lord,
and I yearn for you till my heart is filled with tears.
And though all the world be beautiful,
no earthly thing can occupy my thoughts,
my soul desires only you, O Lord.
  —Saint Silouan of Mount Athos

3.
Jesus Christ: The Prophets' Expectation and Fulfillment

On that day this song will be sung in the land of Judah: We have a strong city; he sets up victory like walls and bulwarks. Open the gates so that the righteous nation that keeps faith may enter in. Those of steadfast mind you keep in peace—in peace because they trust in you. . . . The way of the righteous is level; O Just One, you make smooth the path of the righteous. In the path of your judgments, O LORD, we wait for you; your name and your renown are the soul's desire. My soul yearns for you in the night, my spirit within me earnestly seeks you.

—Isaiah 26:1–3, 7–9

As we get older we tend to think more about our memories from the past than about our unpredictable future. I know I often do so. In the last couple of years, I have found myself yearning more and more for the lessons of the prophets. Their stark, austere presence often awakens something in me, especially during the Advent season. Some of these prophets have become somehow so present, so alive, and so real to me that I keep longing for icons of them in our chapel. I have a great desire, almost a need, to see them visually. An esteem for the prophets has grown in me similar to the one I have for the four Evangelists. I see more and more how well they complement one another. We do have an icon of a prophet in our chapel, Elijah, and it adds a prayerful presence in our place of worship. How I wish our small chapel could also have the presences of Isaiah, Moses, Jeremiah, and especially King David. But even if their icons are missing, we do have their prophetic words in the Scriptures to enlighten our faith and nourish our minds and hearts. Advent, somehow, is an evocative time to quietly listen to the prophets, God's messengers, and to take to heart their message.

Through the messages of the prophets, God slowly began preparing the chosen moment in history in which he would send his only Son, the "Anointed One," the Savior, into the world. From the very beginning God had a plan, and in this plan there is a progression, a gradual revelation of the Messiah in the Old Testament. The prophets, the Lord's true servants, adapted themselves to it—sometimes painfully so—and gave it their complete obedience.

During the preparatory weeks before Christmas, we too are invited to ponder attentively God's plan and to listen to the prophetic words with the ears of our hearts, as Saint Benedict counsels us—not only to listen to the prophets but to go a step further and make their sentiments and messages our own. Our world today longs as much for the Messiah, a Savior, as it did during the times of the prophets. Isaiah beautifully expresses humanity's deep longing for redemption through a personal Savior: "You heavens above, rain down my righteousness; let the clouds shower it down. Let the earth open wide, let salvation spring up, let righteousness flourish with it" (Isa. 45:8 NIV).

In the Gospel of Matthew, we hear the Lord telling his disciples: "For truly I tell you, many prophets and righteous people longed to see what you see but did not see it, and to hear what you hear but did not hear it" (Matt. 13:17 NIV). The prophets and patriarchs of long ago yearned to see the Day of the Lord—that is, to see the arrival and appearance of the Son of God on earth. What the Lord is telling us in very direct words is that what was not given to the prophets to see is given to us through the eyes of faith. We who humbly confess and believe in Christ are given, through faith, the gift of welcoming and embracing the Word made flesh into the very depths of our hearts. This vision of Christ is higher and deeper than all other created reality, and through faith, it is made truly present in our lives.

When I read and meditate on the Gospel account of the Transfiguration of the Lord, I am particularly struck by the presence of two giants from the Old Testament: Moses and Elijah. Their lives prepared the way for the arrival of the Son of God, the Savior. Their presence at Mount Tabor during a most unique, divine event is to witness the fulfillment of their expectations and to behold with their very eyes the presence of him whom they announced long ago, from the beginning of the ages. There is a great distance, physically and historically, between the events at Mount Sinai and Mount Tabor, Mount Horeb and Mount Tabor; but during the glorious moment of Christ's Transfiguration, these distances converge, touch, and signal to each other in witnessing the divine vision—a vision that glows with the endless light of eternity and penetrates into the mystery of God himself. Both prophets and apostles could then claim, paraphrasing Psalm 77, "The mountains saw you, O God, and they were afraid."

Why did Christ lead his disciples onto a high mountain
when he was transfigured in light before them?
It was to show that when disciples arrive
at the summit of love,
they stand out of themselves
and perceive the Invisible One.
Such a person flies over obscure clouds
and comes out into the clear sky of the soul,
and is able to look more acutely
into the Sun of righteousness,
although the perfect vision of the Godhead
always transcends our capacities.
On that day pray in solitude.
For stillness is the mother of prayer,
and prayer is the revelation of the glory of God.
　　　　　　—Saint John Damascene

4.

The Messiah: God's Anointed One

I saw one like a human being coming with the clouds of heaven. And he came to the Ancient One and was presented before him. To him was given dominion and glory and kingship, that all peoples, nations, and languages should serve him. His dominion is an everlasting dominion that shall not pass away, and his kingship is one that shall never be destroyed.

—Daniel 7:13–14

You could describe the Old Testament as the distillation or narrative of early salvation history—in particular, of the long history of the people of Israel. The Israelites, despite being God's chosen people, were in many ways just like others of the surrounding kingdoms: vulnerable, imperfect, weak, at times unfaithful to the Lord. And yet, while at times the Lord might have grown impatient and irritated with Israel's infidelities, he never abandoned his people. In fact, he granted them earthly power and a permanent home, the Promised Land, where he established a sure covenant with them.

God, always a merciful and kind Father, puts up with the frequent mistakes and nonsense of his chosen children. He goes so far as to announce through his prophets a plan for their salvation and redemption. As the prophets reproach the people of Israel for their infidelities, at the very same time they proclaim to them God's great promise: he will send them a Savior of David's long lineage. It is important to acknowledge that the Savior would be a descendant of David, for, like David, he shall become king and prophet, the very essence of the Messiah. In the Hebrew language, Messiah means "he who has received the unction of God's spirit," which, translated into Greek, becomes the word *Christos*—that is, Christ.

It was made known to David that his dynasty shall last forever. Therefore, he prophesies that the Messiah, this descendant of his, will arrive in due time bringing peace and salvation to his people. David calls him "Lord," thus proclaiming the divine origins of the Messiah. From then on, God's covenant with Israel becomes tangible, concrete. It consists on patiently waiting for the "Promised One," the "Anointed One" of God. Henceforth, from generation to generation, a hope in the Messiah becomes the very ethos of the people of Israel. Subsequent prophets continue to announce him, telling the Israelites his time is near—therefore, be prepared! The prophet Micah goes so far as to tell them the Messiah will be born in Bethlehem, as was his ancestor David. And Isaiah provides them a sign, totally unintelligible to them: the young woman shall give birth to a son.

During his lifetime, Christ, our Lord, had a hard time convincing his contemporaries that he was indeed the expected, anointed Messiah. For the Jews of Jesus's time were convinced that the Messiah, the Anointed One of God, would liberate the Jewish people and restore the kingdom of Israel. Christ presented himself as something very different. How, then, could many of the Jews believe he was the Messiah? Slowly but surely the Lord tried to convey that his mission was not to restore the kingdom of Israel, but to forge a new covenant. With it, those who gained new life through him would sit with him one day at the right hand of God. During Christ's lifetime, it was mostly the apostles who attributed the title "Messiah" to the Lord, as when Andrew introduced Jesus to his brother Peter saying, "'We have found the Messiah' (which is translated Anointed)" (John 1:41). In another instance, when the Samaritan woman approaches Jesus, she tells him, "'I know that Messiah is coming' (who is called Christ). 'When he comes, he will proclaim all things to us.'" And Jesus responds to her, "I am he, the one who is speaking to you" (John 4:25–26).

If Jesus used the title "Messiah" sparingly because of its political connotations, which were of no interest to him, he never denied it either. He only used it in the sense that served his divine purposes. Jesus was perfectly conscious that he was the Christ, the Messiah, but he widened the concept and gave to it a true spiritual and universal significance: he was the Messiah, the Anointed One of God, who came not as a liberator of Israel, but as a Savior to establish a new kingdom of God and to reconcile humanity to God.

From our forefathers, the patriarchs and prophets of the Old Testament, we have learned that the Scriptures are not a series of speculations about metaphysical truths, such as how creation came about or how or when the end of the world shall take place. The Scriptures—as proclaimed, lived, and explained by our ancestors in the faith—are more an interpretation of divine history, the tale of God inserting himself into it for the sake of saving sinful humanity, the very work of his hands.

In the fullness of time, when God sent the Promised One into our world, his only Son, the Messiah, there were many who did not recognize him. When Jesus assigned to himself the messianic title by proclaiming the first time he preached, "Today this prophecy is here fulfilled," it was anathema to those present in his hometown Nazareth synagogue. Centuries have run their course since. We know the Messiah has come and will come again at the end of time, and we can find great consolation in it.

To prophets promised long ago,
and born before the birth of light,
Whom Gabriel announced with joy,
the Lord himself comes down to earth.
In lowly guise the Most High comes
to save the world which sin had lost.
    —"Verbum Salutis," anonymous tenth-century hymn

5.

God's Timeless Plan: The Incarnation

For God so loved the world that he gave his only Son, so that everyone who believes in him may not perish but may have eternal life.

—John 3:16

I have learned from the Prophet, who foretold in older times the coming of Emmanuel, that a certain holy Virgin should bear a child. Now I long to know how the nature of mortal men shall undergo union with the Godhead.

—Byzantine Matins of the Annunciation

Habitually, during the days of the Advent season, we plunge ourselves deeper than usual into the mystery of the Incarnation. After all, the Advent and Christmas seasons are all about this wonderful and inexplicable mystery. When silently meditating upon it, I always feel awestruck by the ever-strange beauty of the mystery, its majestic and overwhelming power. Everything about the way the Lord went about accomplishing his mystery is beyond our human comprehension. Only the gift of faith can give us a glimpse into that unfathomable abyss.

It all has to do with the Father's plans to send his only Son into a world he created—a world that often dissented from God's original plan, and thus was in desperate need of redemption. The angel Gabriel, bearer of good news, announces God's plan to Mary: by the mysterious action of the Holy Spirit, she will bear a son, the Son of the Most High, and through him both new hope and eternal salvation are being offered by God to the world. In this strange and awesome mystery, humanity and divinity are now joined in Mary's womb. At the unique and crucial moment of the Incarnation, the course of human history changes forever: the Word of God, the Logos, is made flesh and he dwells among us. *Et Verbum caro factum est et habitavit in nobis.*

The mystery of the Incarnation thus begins at a very precise moment in time and history: when Mary utters her *fiat*, or assent, to God's plan. Mary, of course, was familiar with the words of the prophet Isaiah: "Behold, a virgin shall conceive, and bear a son, and his name shall be called Emmanuel" (Isa. 7:14 DRA). What she did not know until then is that Isaiah was speaking of her. As one of the lovely Gregorian antiphons sung during Advent tells us, "This is the good news the prophets foretold: the Savior will be born of the Virgin Mary."

The Greek Fathers are well known for their excellent homilies on the mystery of the Incarnation. Nothing can really surpass their poetic realism in trying to explain what God accomplished in our midst, on behalf of all of us. The following is a paraphrase of a sermon on the subject by our father among the saints, Saint Gregory Nazianzus:

> The very Son of God, who existed before the ages, he is the invisible one, the incomprehensible, the incorporeal, the beginning of beginning, the light of light, the fountain of life and immortality, the image of the archetype, the immovable seal, the perfect resemblance, the definition and living word of the Father; he it is who comes to his own image and embraces our nature for the good of our own nature and unites himself to an intelligent soul for the good of my soul, to purify like by like. The Son of God absorbs in himself all that is human, except sin. He is conceived in the womb of the Virgin Mary, who had been first prepared in soul and body by the Holy Spirit; his birth is treated with honor, and virginity is received with new honor. He comes forth as God, in the human nature he has absorbed, one being, made of two opposite elements, flesh and spirit; spirit gives diversity, flesh receives it.
>
> He who is wealth itself is made poor; he takes on the poverty of our flesh that we may gain the wealth of his divinity. He who is fullness in himself accepts to become empty; he empties himself for a brief period of time, that we all may share in his fullness. We need God to take our flesh and die that we might love. We died with him that we may be purified. We rise again with him, because we have died with him.

We are glorified with him, because we have risen again with him.

The more I immerse myself, humbly, prayerfully, into the mystery of God's Incarnation, the more I discover something about its author and accomplisher: the Holy Spirit. It is through humble prayer and the grace of the Holy Spirit that we fathom something of that otherwise incomprehensible mystery, an inkling about the two different natures of Christ: divine and human. Only the Holy Spirit can communicate to the praying believer a hint of that splendid divine union between two different natures and wills. Infused divine knowledge is a rare and special gift from the Holy Spirit. Only his grace can awaken in our hearts and minds this sort of knowledge. It is through experiencing the Holy Spirit interiorly, deep within our souls, that the mystery of the Incarnate Word, the person of Jesus Christ, slowly gets revealed to us. And only the Holy Spirit, the very author of the mystery, can deign to confer on us the necessary faith and grace to arrive at this blessed and divine knowledge.

> *Be born in us,*
> *Incarnate Love.*
> *Take our flesh and blood and*
> *give us your humanity;*
> *Take our eyes and*
> *give us your vision.*
> *Take our minds and*
> *give us your pure thoughts.*

Take our feet and
set them in your path.
Take our hands and
Fold them in your prayer.
Take our hearts and
give them your will to love.
—Caryll Houselander

6.

Emmanuel: God with Us

O Emmanuel, our King and Lawgiver,
The long-awaited hope of the nations,
Savior of all people;
O come, our Lord and God,
Set free the people whom You love.
> —"O Emmanuel" from the "O Antiphons"
> (Vespers, Dec. 23)

Each year on the evening of December 23, we praise the Lord with the last of our Advent vespers. The final of the great "O Antiphons" is sung. Already at Lauds, during our morning praise, the liturgy forecasting the Good News tells us to ready ourselves (*Ecce completa sunt*), and so we sing joyfully, "Behold, all things are accomplished." This refers to those things spoken by the angel concerning the Virgin Mary. As the bells ring during the singing of the last "O Antiphon" and the Magnificat, we draw deeply into ourselves once more, knowing now with certainty that the prophecies of long ago are soon to be fulfilled.

O Emmanuel, our King and Lawgiver,
The long-awaited hope of the nations . . .

For the first time during the Advent season we call upon the one who is coming with the name given to him by the angel: Emmanuel, meaning "God with us." We recall also the words of the prophet Isaiah: "The young woman, pregnant and about to bear a son, shall name him Emmanuel." The very meaning of the name reveals to us the depth and tenderness of God's love for us. He wants to be one of us, to dwell and remain with us as always. He desires to share our human nature, and he wants us to share in his divine life. Indeed, he is the "Lover of mankind," as the Eastern liturgy frequently calls him. With his coming among us, we stand in awe as "the grace of God has appeared, bringing salvation for all people" (Titus 2:11 ESV). The long-awaited hope of all nations is soon to be rewarded and fulfilled.

> *O come, our Lord and God,*
> *Set free the people whom You love.*

When Christmas Day arrives after the obscure depths and mystery of the holy night, Emmanuel, the Christ child, is born unto us. God appears on earth, and he is in truth one with us. All peoples of the earth are called to acknowledge that he, Emmanuel, is indeed the Messiah, the Anointed One of God, and therefore all of us must submit to him. Christ-Emmanuel is the Light of the World, and he comes to free us from the darkness we are engulfed in. He comes to make us free and invites us to share in his very life. We submit in complete freedom and joy, for in his infinite love he came to save us, to rescue us, to be one with us!

God is with us!
Understand, all you nations,
And submit yourselves,
For God is with us!
—Byzantine anthem sung throughout
  the Christmas season

7.

Jesus, the Prince of Peace

For a child is born to us, a son is given to us;
upon his shoulder dominion rests.
They name him Wonder-Counselor, God-Hero,
Father-Forever, Prince of Peace.
>   —Isaiah 9:5 (NABRE)

And suddenly there was a multitude of the heavenly host
with the angel, praising God and saying: "Glory to God
in the highest and on earth peace to those on whom his
favor rests."
>   —Luke 2:13–14 (NABRE)

It is a critical fact, and yet most Christians never completely acknowledge it: from the very beginning, from the prophets on, the person of the Messiah was always announced as a messenger of peace. Isaiah, in speaking of the coming Messiah, proclaims a new era of great peace and goes so far as to call him a "prince of peace." On the day of the Lord's Nativity we hear once again the same message in the angels' singing: "Glory to God in the highest and peace to those on whom his favor rests." Peace, not conflict, violence, or war—the true peace that descends from heaven—is the trademark of the Messiah. And yet today, just as in the time of Christ, we are surrounded by ruthless wars approved by our politicians—endless death in the name of those who represent us. Could all this be in accord with the message of the Prince of Peace? Could he approve of this ghastly, inhuman behavior? These are questions an honest disciple of Christ is compelled to ask.

There is no doubt in my mind that Christ opposes every form of human violence. He plainly rebuked his disciples when they tried to defend him, saying, "All who take the sword will perish by the sword." The Lord, good master that he was, never minced words, and the apostles and early disciples of the Lord understood this correctly. It is said of Saint Martin of Tours, a soldier in the Roman army, that once he was baptized a Christian, he laid down his sword. When he was asked why, he responded simply that now as a soldier of Christ he could no longer bear arms or kill anyone. In the Gospels, the recourse to violence is never acceptable. To early Christians the Lord's teachings were plain, clear, and simple. There was no room for reinterpreting. And they heard Isaiah's prophetic words:

> They shall beat their swords into plowshares
> and their spears into pruning hooks;
> One nation shall not raise the sword against another,
> nor shall they train for war again. (Isa. 2:4 NABRE)

When Pope Paul VI came to the United Nations in New York City, he pleaded with the people of all nations to stop all wars and recourses to war. He cried out, *"Jamais plus la guerre!"* ("War, never again. Never!") He was not sending a personal message; he was pleading for the message of the Gospel to be heard. He was not saying this in his own name, but in the name of Christ whom he represented. He was asking all people to choose the way of nonviolence and to walk along the path of peace traced by Christ, our master. By opposing all violence and instead living in harmony and peace with others—even our so-called enemies—we make a direct choice to foster and extend the kingdom of God, the only true kingdom. Saint Paul is explicit about this: "The kingdom of God is not a matter of food and drink, but of righteousness, peace, and joy in the holy Spirit; whoever serves Christ in this way is pleasing to God and approved by others. Let us then pursue what leads to peace and to building up one another" (Rom. 14:17–19 NABRE).

Our Christian hope is a clear invitation from the Lord to become instruments of his peace, true peacemakers. In the Sermon on the Mount, we hear the Lord proclaim: "Blessed are the peacemakers, for they will be called children of God" (Matt. 5:9 NIV). This is simply the same message conveyed by the angels on that first Christmas night. To become in truth a Christian peacemaker, after the example of the Lord himself, we must accept the risk of being controversial, countercultural, and taken as a fool by others, just like many of Jesus's disciples before us: Saint Martin of Tours, Saint Benedict, the Desert Fathers and Mothers, Saint Francis of Assisi, and in our days, servant of God Dorothy Day, Thomas Merton, and others. All of these people have been rejected often because of their evangelical views and examples. It was the price they paid for true discipleship. It takes a profound faith in God's words and promises, a fierce inner fortitude, and plenty of God's grace to accept the challenge to become a peacemaker like Christ. Indeed, to follow our model and master by working for peace entails pursuing reconciliation among all people—among those hostile to each other; among nations at war; among family, neighbors, and churches in discord. There is nothing romantic about being a true peacemaker. It involves hard work, dying to self daily, fidelity to prayer, extreme humility, and total obedience to God's word. Only by doing this can we become, in the words of Saint Francis of Assisi, "instruments of his peace."

Our challenge, as Christians, is to honor the Prince of Peace by renewing our commitment to the Christmas message sung by the angels, and by doing everything possible to foster and implement peace and harmony among all the people of the earth, for he who comes as Savior of all is also the Prince of Peace to all.

Lord, make me an instrument of Your peace.
Where there is hatred, let me sow love;
where there is injury, pardon;
where there is doubt, faith;
where there is despair, hope;
where there is darkness, light;
where there is sadness, joy.
O, Divine Master,

grant that I may not so much seek to be consoled as to
console;
to be understood as to understand;
to be loved as to love;
for it is in giving that we receive;
it is in pardoning that we are pardoned;
it is in dying that we are born again to eternal life.
—Prayer of Saint Francis of Assisi

8.

Jesus, the Lamb of God

Abraham said, "God himself will provide the lamb for a burnt offering, my son." So the two of them walked on together.

—Genesis 22:8

But I was like a gentle lamb led to the slaughter. And I did not know it was against me that they devised schemes, saying, "Let us destroy the tree with its fruit, let us cut him off from the land of the living, so that his name will no longer be remembered."

—Jeremiah 11:19

The next day [John] saw Jesus coming toward him, and said, "Behold, the Lamb of God, who takes away the sins of the world!"

—John 1:29 (ESV)

You know that you were ransomed from the futile ways inherited from your ancestors, not with perishable things like silver or gold, but with the precious blood of Christ, like that of a lamb without defect or blemish.

—1 Peter 1:18–19

Each year in our small monastery, as we enter into the mysteries of Holy Week, we repeat and reenter the Holy City of Jerusalem, where great things shall happen shortly. Much of the mystery lived during these holy days has to do with celebrating and reliving the events of the Lord's Passover, his saving passion and resurrection. Coincidentally, about the same time each year the ewes in our monastic sheepfold give birth to tiny little lambs. They serve to remind us vividly of the true Passover Lamb, whose memory is being honored during those days. We recall then the words of an ancient church father, Saint Melito of Sardis: "Christ was led forth like a lamb; He was slaughtered like a sheep. He ransomed Israel from the land of Egypt. He freed us from our slavery to the devil as He freed Israel from the hand of Pharaoh. He sealed our souls with his true spirit and the members of our body with his own blood. . . . He was sacrificed in the Passover lamb." Indeed, Jesus, our meek and humble Redeemer, is the true paschal Lamb, to whose supper we are all invited. For our sake, he offered himself to the Father during the very time of the Jewish Passover, at the precise moment when the paschal lambs were being slaughtered in sacrificial offering in the Temple. Christ's self-offering, which took place once and for all time, was accomplished out of that ineffable and incomprehensible love of his so that he might wash away the sins of us all and bring salvation to the entire world.

The designation "Lamb of God" is an official sacrificial title. Sacrificial lambs played a unique role in the Old Testament, all throughout the old covenant. Again and again in the books of Genesis and Exodus and the prophets Isaiah and Jeremiah, we hear references to sacrificial lambs. It is therefore clearly understood when Christ, God's immaculate Lamb, makes his entrance into our world, that a sacrificial system had been previously arranged by the Lord himself.

In the Old Testament account of the Passover feast, the first thing we encounter is a description of the sacrificial Passover lamb. In reading this sacred text, we again see how the innocent sacrificial lamb becomes a symbolic remembrance of God's deliverance for the people of Israel. The sacrifice of the Passover lamb and the sprinkling of the blood on the doorsteps of the houses of Egypt becomes then a rich symbol of Christ's atonement on the cross. Those for whom he died shall later partake of the sacrificial supper of the Lamb, for they are now redeemed and cleansed by the blood of God's immaculate Lamb. The angel of death shall henceforth have no power to harm them. They are forever sealed and protected by the blood of the Lamb.

We must see the announcement by John the Baptist that Jesus is the Lamb of God who takes away the sins of the world in the context of the prophecies of the Old Testament. The one John addressed as "Lamb of God" is the same later proclaimed by the apostle Paul: "Christ, our paschal lamb, has been sacrificed." John knew well the ancient prophecies, the role of the sacrificial lamb in the history of the people of Israel, and he did not hesitate in the least to equate the sacrificial lamb of the prophets with the slaughtered Lamb to come. This time, however, the Lamb is sacrificed not in a temple or household, but on the wood of the cross, neutralizing in his own flesh the sins of the world.

O holy and blameless Lamb of God, our true Passover Lamb and long-suffering Lord, for our sake you accepted death on a Cross; glory to you.

Worthy is the Lamb who was slain, to receive power and wealth and wisdom and might and honor and glory and blessing! . . . To him who sits on the throne and to the Lamb be blessing and honor and glory and might forever and ever!

—Rev. 5:12b, 13b (ESV)

9.

Christ, the Lord

The LORD will reign forever and ever.
—Exodus 15:18

Who is the King of Glory?
The LORD, strong and mighty,
The LORD, mighty in battle. . . .
Who is this King of Glory?
The LORD of hosts,
he is the King of Glory.
—Psalm 24:8, 10

This was in accordance with the eternal purpose that he has carried out in Christ Jesus our Lord, in whom we have access to God in boldness and confidence through faith in him.
—Ephesians 3:11–12

To understand why, from early on in the New Testament and church tradition, Christ has been addressed as *Adonai,* or Lord, consider that for the Israelites, it was forbidden to refer to God by name, Yahweh. Because this was considered blasphemous, Israelites started substituting *Adonai.*

The name "Lord" inspired reverence, respect, fear, majesty, and glory, and thus it became an acceptable substitute. Also, Lord (*Kyrios* in Greek) carries a more familiar, more intimate connotation—it indicates an attitude of closeness to him whom we worship.

In the Scriptures, especially the works of apostles Saint John and Saint Paul, it is clear that Christ is the loving image of God the Father and equal to him in all things. If he is equal to the Father in his divinity, then he is also worthy of worship and adoration, as is his Father in heaven. It is understandable, then, that Christ is referred to as Lord or *Kyrios* in the simple sense of that word.

Our Christian faith is based on the confession that Christ is Lord. Peter doesn't hesitate to proclaim Jesus as such while preaching to the people of Israel: "Therefore let the entire house of Israel know with certainty that God has made him both Lord and Messiah, this Jesus who you crucified" (Acts 2:36). Our faith, a gift from the Holy Spirit, teaches us that Christ possesses complete lordship over all creation; over the church, which is his body; and over each of us who were ransomed by his blood.

Long before the time of the Incarnation, God created the world through the Word. "All things were created through him and for him. And he is before all things, and in him all things hold together" (Col. 1:16–17 ESV). From the very first instant of creation, the Father offers the eternal Word, the Son, complete lordship and possession over creation, the work of his hands. In time, by the power of the Holy Spirit, the Word takes flesh from creation itself, thus becoming, in the words of Saint Paul, "the firstborn of all creation" (Col. 1:15 ESV).

Jesus's lordship over the community of the faithful, the church, is perfectly understandable since this church is his body, and he gained complete control over his body by his death on the cross. Asserting his lordship, Christ provides us with the presence of the Holy Spirit, so that it may equip us to grow into our full realization as the body of Christ and reach perfect maturity to the measure of the full stature of Christ, as Saint Paul tells us (Eph. 4:13). The grace and help from the Holy Spirit is essential to Jesus' lordship over his body, the church, for as Saint Paul proclaims, "no one can say, 'Jesus is Lord,' except by the Holy Spirit" (1 Cor. 12:3b).

And last but not least, Christ's lordship over each one of us is based on his redemptive act of salvation from which each of us benefits individually. Christ, our Lord, calls each of us, regardless of background, to partake of a new life in God, eating the bread of his body and drinking the cup of his blood, thus proclaiming again and again the Lord's death until the time of his return. Indeed, Christ is both our Lord and Savior, and all of us who accept his lordship over us and worship him daily in spirit and truth are united to him and the Father forever by the grace and power of the Holy Spirit.

You are worthy, our Lord and God,
to receive glory and honor and power,
for you created all things,
and by your will they existed and were created.
—Revelation 4:11

10.

Christ, Son of the Living God

Now when Jesus came into the district of Ceasaria Philippi, he asked his disciples, "Who do people say that the Son of Man is?" And they said, "Some say John the Baptist, others say Elijah, and others Jeremiah or one of the prophets." He said to them, "But who do you say that I am?" Simon Peter replied, "You are the Christ, the Son of the living God." And Jesus answered him, "Blessed are you, Simon Bar-Jonah! For flesh and blood has not revealed this to you, but my Father who is in heaven."

—Matthew 16:13–17 (ESV)

For he received honor and glory from God the Father when that voice was conveyed to him by the Majestic Glory, saying, "This is my Son, my Beloved, with whom I am well pleased." We ourselves heard this voice coming from heaven, while we were with him on the holy mountain.

—2 Peter 1:17–18

Saint Cyril of Alexandria, in his treatise *Against Those Who Are Unwilling to Confess that the Holy Virgin Is*

Theotokos, clearly states that Christ is "eternally God who has also become man."[3] He is, he continues, "eternally the Logos and Light and Brightness of the Father, and he possesses the sovereignty of the God-befitting glory." Christ assumed the name "Son," says Saint Cyril, "at His Incarnation, when he became man." Christ is God by nature, and he remains thus when at the Incarnation he accepts and takes on the human condition. During Christ's baptism in the Jordan, the Lord received the extraordinary testimony from the Father, whose voice was heard proclaiming Christ to be his beloved Son. How could anyone doubt afterward Jesus's divine sonship?

As a normal human being, Christ's growth in knowledge and wisdom was gradual; in the same way, he grew gradually into the full awareness of his divine sonship. Already at around age twelve, when Mary and Joseph find him teaching in the temple and he is questioned as to what he is doing, he replies to them straightforwardly: "Why were you searching for me? Did you not know that I must be in my Father's house?" (Lk. 2:49). He already possessed the intimate knowledge of being the Father's only Son. Later on, during the three years of his public ministry, he would perform signs and wonders before the people of Israel, always acknowledging that as Son of the living God, he was foremost seeking the glory of his Father. Throughout the Gospels, Christ never seeks to act for himself; in all things he tries to accomplish his Father's will. He remains the obedient Son of God, obedient to his Father to the end, even to death on the cross.

The title "Son of the living God" indicates Jesus's direct and very unique relationship to God, his Father. He cherished the divine reality contained in that assumption, and he expressed it beautifully in John's Gospel: "I do as the Father has commanded me, so that the world may know that I love the Father" (John 14:31). Jesus, as Son of the living God, is coequal to his Father, who loves him, calling him "beloved Son" and finding all his pleasure in him. Ultimately, it is this divine realization of sonship that compels the Lord to empty himself and become a servant in complete obedience to the Father who loves him. This obedience is later rewarded by the Father, who highly glorifies him by returning him to his previous state of glory, the one he possessed from all eternity, before the creation of the world, where he is seated at the Father's right hand (see Phil. 2:5–11).

In monastic life, getting to know Christ by the pure grace of the Holy Spirit, worshiping and acknowledging him as the Son of the living God, is our joy, our peace, and our weapon against every form of evil. We monks remain basically poor, sinful, and lonely, and only by making recourse to the Son of the living God, Christ our Savior, can we free ourselves from endless, trivial concerns and direct the total attention of both our hearts and minds toward him who is the true life.

O Lord and Savior,
in your green pastures, give peace to our restless hearts.
You are our Shepherd, and we are your flock.
Refresh our souls in your living waters,
the waters that provide serenity to our souls.

Amid temptations to wander, keep us in the right path.
During our days in the dark valley, enlighten our steps.
Lead us all to the banquet of life,
where you offer the cup of salvation
to all those who thirst and hunger for you.

11.

Christ, the Good Shepherd

The LORD is my shepherd, I shall not want.

He makes me lie down in green pastures;

He leads me beside still waters;

He restores my soul.

He leads me in right paths for his name's sake.

—Psalm 23:1–3

I myself will be the shepherd of my sheep, and I will make them lie down, says the Lord GOD. I will seek the lost, and I will bring back the strayed, and I will bind up the injured, and I will strengthen the weak, but the fat and the strong I will destroy. I will feed them with justice.

—Ezekiel 34:15–16

I am the good shepherd. I know my own and my own know me, just as the Father knows me and I know the Father. And I lay down my life for the sheep. I have other sheep that do not belong to the fold. I must bring them also, and they will listen to my voice. So there will be one flock, one shepherd.

—John 10:14–16

One of the most beautiful points of convergence of Old and New Testaments is the Lord describing himself as a shepherd—a good shepherd—in both. It is a metaphor for God's tenderness toward all his children, his sheep, whom he looks after with exquisite, loving care, seeing that we are fed as a true shepherd would, and carrying the lambs, the most vulnerable among us, in his arms to protect them from predators (see Isa. 40:11). The image of the Good Shepherd in the Scriptures also resembles the reality of a mother's tenderness for her young infant. Jesus, the Good Shepherd, wanted to make all of this clear to his sheep, his followers.

I have always loved the Gospel of John in its entirety, but I have been particularly attracted to chapter 10, where the Lord describes in exquisite detail the nature and role of the Good Shepherd—and, of course, the responsibility he assumes for each of us, his sheep, going as far as to be ready to give his life for the least among us. Christ, the Good Shepherd, in John 10, wishes not to lose a single one of his sheep. He makes every effort to retrieve the lost ones, even those who do not belong to his fold. For the Good Shepherd, saving the lives of any one of his sheep is worth the supreme self-oblation the Father demanded of him. He clearly understands this demand, and in his love for the Father and for his flock, he asserts: "I am the good shepherd. The good shepherd lays down his life for the sheep" (John 10:11).

Believers and nonbelievers may sometimes ask why Jesus used the image of a shepherd and his sheep to explain God's boundless love for each of us, his creatures. In the Middle Eastern and Mediterranean cultures, the local people understood well what a shepherd did and what shepherding was all about. Principally, the role of the shepherd was to care for his sheep and lambs, provide them with good pasture land and necessary water, ensure they have adequate protection from predators, and go off after any that wander from the flock. The intimate and loving way the shepherd cared for and related to his sheep was totally in sync with Jesus's mind and heart. I can't resist but to quote here another passage from John's Gospel. This beautiful text illustrates in great depth Jesus's supreme concern for his sheep, each of us, even at the moment of his imminent departure to the Father, just before his ascension:

> When they had finished breakfast, Jesus said to Simon Peter, "Simon son of John, do you love me more than these?" He said to him, "Yes, Lord; you know I love you." Jesus said, "Feed my lambs." A second time he said to him, "Simon son of John, do you love me?" He said to him, "Yes, Lord; you know that I love you." Jesus said to him, "Tend my sheep." He said to him the third time, "Simon son of John, do you love me?" Peter felt hurt because he said to him the third time, "Do you love me?" And he said to him, "Lord, you know everything; you know that I love you." Jesus said to him, "Feed my sheep" (John 21:15–17).

In the image of Christ, the Good Shepherd, we are confronted once again with the ultimate mystery: Christ is true man and true God. God came into our world in Christ, but he came as man. As man he was man, and as God he was God. In his infinite mercy, as the Good Shepherd of our souls, he protects and draws all of us to himself, where he is one with the Father and the Holy Spirit. In the face of Christ, our Shepherd, we encounter the reality of the mystery: Christ alone is truth, and he is also life and love. In his immense, infinite love for us, he gives all of himself to us; and now it is our turn to return our complete selves, all our limited and complete love, to him. The more strongly our love for him takes hold in us, the more we open ourselves to his truth and life. As we live our lives, day in and day out, we hold on to his final promise: "A little while longer, and I shall return again."

Give ear, O Shepherd of Israel,
You who lead Joseph like a flock!
You who are enthroned upon the cherubim, shine forth
before Ephraim and Benjamin and Manasseh.
Stir up your might,
and come to save us!
Restore us, O God;
let your face shine, that we may be saved.
—Psalm 80:1–3

12.

Christ, the Door and
Keeper of the Gate

*I have left an open door before you, which no one can
close.*

—Revelation 3:8 (NABRE)

*Enter through the narrow gate; for the gate is wide and
the road is easy that leads to destruction, and there are
many who take it. For the gate is narrow and the road
is hard that leads to life, and there are few who find it.*

—Matthew 7:13–14

*Listen! I am standing at the door, knocking; if you hear
my voice and open the door, I will come in to you and
eat with you, and you with me.*

—Revelation 3:20

During the year, I use different images of Christ provided
to us in the Scriptures, particularly the Gospels, to feed
my inner prayer. One of the images that is very personal
and speaks volumes to me is the one of Christ the door,
the keeper of the gate. Very often when I pray or meditate

gazing at the large icon of the Lord in our chapel, I get a clear and distinct understanding that Christ is truly the door through which we must all pass to arrive to the Father. As I focus on that precise icon day after day, I see as it were a wide opening at the very center of Christ's image, an open door through which I must go to enter deeply into God. In the icon, the Lord remains totally still in his mystery, his majesty, inviting me lovingly to come to him, to enter into him, so to speak, so that he may show me the Father. He gently reminds me again and again that "he who sees Me sees the Father" for "I and the Father are one."

In the stark reality of the icon, as in the Gospels, one can hear Christ telling us again and again to gather our scattered inner faculties and to channel ourselves in his direction, into that wide open door which is himself: "Very truly, I tell you, anyone who does not enter the sheepfold by the gate but climbs in by another way is a thief and a bandit. The one who enters by the gate is the shepherd of the sheep. The gatekeeper opens the gate for him, and the sheep hear his voice. . . . Very truly, I tell you, I am the gate for the sheep. . . . I am the gate. Whoever enters by me will be saved, and will come in and go out and find pasture" (John 10:1–9).

Christ shows us the way, and he is the Way. Christ gives us the light, and he is the Light. Christ is the door that opens into the light. The door and gate are narrow, but they open into the sheepfold, and the Shepherd is there at the gate, awaiting us, his flock, ready to lead us inside. He reminds us that he is the gate to the Father's kingdom, the only one,

and that we are all invited to pass through the gate, himself,
to reach our final destination.

From where do You come?
How do you enter?
I mean, within my cell, completely closed on all sides?
For this is indeed something strange, beyond word or
thought.
But that You are with me,
suddenly whole and brilliantly shining
and You are seen under the form of a light,
as the moon in full brilliance,
this leaves me thoughtless and speechless, my God!
I know that You are
the one who has come to enlighten
all who sit in darkness.
I am beyond myself;
I am beyond senses and words
at seeing this strange wonder
which surpasses all creation,
every nature, every word.
> —Saint Symeon the New Theologian,
> Hymn 29, *Hymns of Divine Love*

13.

Jesus: The Holy Name

Save me, O God, by your name
and vindicate me by your might.
—Psalm 54:1

The name of the LORD *is a strong tower;*
the righteous run into it and are safe.
—Proverbs 18:10

I will give, in my house, and within my walls,
a monument and a name
better than sons and daughters;
I will give them an everlasting name
that shall not be cut off.
—Isaiah 56:5

Very truly, I tell you, if you ask anything of the Father in
my name, he will give it to you.
—John 16:23

Whatever you do, in word or deed, do everything in the
name of the Lord Jesus, giving thanks to God the Father
through him.
—Colossians 3:17

The discovery of the holy name of Jesus, its frequent invocation in prayer, is a powerful means for Christians to enter ever more deeply into the mystery of the Incarnation. The name was chosen by the Father from all eternity and first uttered and transmitted to his perplexed Mother-to-be during the angel Gabriel's very special visit, the Annunciation. From the very first moment of the Word's conception in Mary's womb, the person and the name are identified as one: Jesus, which means "God saves" in Hebrew. The Word is made flesh; God becomes man, and he is given the saving name of Jesus, thus making it clear to all that Jesus is the Savior, he who comes to save.

In ancient times, among the Israelites and some of the pagans, the name of a god represented the person and character of that particular deity. It was believed then that each god was totally present in his or her name. The name of the god brought his or her real presence into the heart of the worshiper. Thus, it was considered natural that by praying and repeating the name of a particular god, the believer was standing in that god's real presence. From these prayers and repetitions, believers conjectured that special blessings would follow.

The early Christians inherited this tradition from the Jewish people, and from early on they began praying by using the holy name of Jesus. Because of this practice, these Christians were often described by others as the "People of the Name." Then and now, the name of Jesus makes us aware not only that he is present, but that he is present as Savior—which is what the word *Jesus* signifies. He is Savior, both as the Author of salvation and as the one who offers salvation to each of us. The book of Acts strongly affirms: "There is salvation in no one else, for there is no other name under heaven given among mortals by which we must be saved" (Acts 4:12).

The invocation of the sacred name of Jesus connects us directly to that other fundamental reality of the person of Christ: his intrinsic relationship to his Father. In the first chapter of the Gospel of John, we read: "In the beginning was the Logos, the Word." This Logos is the person of Jesus, the Word spoken by the Father from all eternity. The Father loves his Son, and pours out all his love into this beloved, and through him onto all of us who are as branches humbly united to Jesus, the true vine.

In honoring and invoking Jesus's name, we enter not only into the person of Jesus and his salvation, but into the mysterious communion of the Father and the Son. As he assures us, "I am in the Father and the Father is in me" (John 14:11), and "Whoever has seen me has seen the Father" (John 14:9).

In everyday life, the invocation of the name of Jesus brings the Lord directly into our hearts and minds. His sacred name is the bearer of his person. We must eagerly and frequently pray the holy name, realizing deeply that it is the very substance of his person. Now and for all eternity, the sacred name represents Jesus's real presence and his innermost reality in God.

O God,
Who did appoint your only begotten Son
to be the Redeemer of mankind,
and did command that his name
should be called Jesus:
Mercifully grant me,
who venerates his holy name on earth,
to likewise attain the fruition
of beholding him in heaven.
—Prayer to the Holy Name of Jesus

PART II

CHRIST
in the Gospel Tradition

14.

Christ, the Lord of History

"Behold, I am making all things new."
—Revelation 21:5 (ESV)

That He might fill all things with Himself.
—Liturgy of Saint Basil

Among the liturgical seasons, Advent has a special message. It points us directly to Christ, our Redeemer and Savior, the Lord who is to come. He is the Alpha and the Omega, the beginning and the end, indeed the Lord of history. The ages, time, and the seasons were created by him and for him alone, for at the appointed time the Father sent his only begotten Son to rule over all. We Christians live in the here and now, but the movement and progress of time looks to its ultimate consummation when all things will converge in Christ. Saint Paul reminds us that every nation, and each of us, is made and called to belong to Christ alone; therefore, we must place all our hope in him.

Our finite, time-limited existence is caught in that patient waiting for the Mystery to be revealed at the end in all its fullness. This is why Advent references not only Christ's first coming into history, but even more so his ultimate coming at the end of the ages, when he shall appear in the clouds as our Judge and Savior, and when human history shall again be reshaped and made new by him. At the end, at the closing of the ages, time itself shall find its culmination in Christ's eternal reality, in his fullness; for indeed, he alone is the Lord, and the only purpose of all history. "Behold, indeed, I come to make all things new."

> *Grant us, O Lord, to cling to You,*
> *not in our outward beings*
> *but in our hidden selves,*
> *and may we follow You*
> *until we behold your face.*
> *For in this world, Lord,*
> *a person continues to follow after You*
> *as he becomes perfected,*
> *but in the world to come*
> *You will manifest your very face to him:*
> *then he will no longer be traveling after You,*
> *but will be with You*
> *in the Kingdom.*
> —Prayer of John of Apamea, Syriac monk

15.

Jesus of Bethlehem:
A Light Shines in the Darkness

A bright Light shines in the darkness:
Rejoice and be glad, O Bethlehem, land of Judea,
For in you the Lord shall shine forth as the dawn.
Give ear, you mountains and hills
And all lands surrounding Judea;
For Christ is coming to save the people
He has created and whom he loves.
—Byzantine Vespers, Sunday before the Nativity

Blessed be he who possesses Bethlehem in his heart,
and in whose heart Christ is born daily.
—Saint Jerome

Every one of us was born in Bethlehem, which became
the birthplace of redeemed humanity.
—Matthew the Poor

Each year, during our dread and dark days of winter, the Christmas season provides the occasion to contemplate and reflect on the mystery of the God who became flesh for our sake. In his infinite love for humanity, God, the Word made flesh, assumed our nature and allowed us, for the first time, to gaze upon his own human face. Faith opens our inner eyes to the wonder of the Christmas mystery: Christ's birth in Bethlehem of Judea. Our faith directs our steps to that special place, thus revealing to us the mystery we celebrate and proclaim at Christmas in the marvelous exchange sung in the antiphon "*O admirabile commercium*" ("O Wonderful Exchange"). This antiphon describes the marrying of divinity from on high with poor, sinful humanity here below. This wedding, this unique transformation we speak of as the Incarnation, is accomplished by Jesus and becomes visible at the moment of his birth. The sweet and humble infant we contemplate in the créche is the wondrous link that unites heaven and earth. The mystery of Bethlehem, we are reminded, unfolds before our eyes in the Lord's birth from a humble virgin, a birth to accomplish precisely the work of our salvation. Indeed, O wondrous mystery!

Usually, there is a great deal of rich symbolism contained in liturgical celebrations. For instance, it is the custom in many parts of the world to celebrate Christmas Matins and the Divine Liturgy in the middle of a (usually) cold, dark winter night. There is a logical connection between this late-night celebration and the event itself. As an ancient liturgical Christmas text describes the event, "While all things were in deep silence, and the night was in the midst of her course, your almighty Word leapt down from heaven, from your royal throne, O Lord" ("Dum medium silentium," *Divine Office*, antiphon for January 1, Christmas octave). If we await a Savior's arrival during the darkest hours of night, it is to remind us of our own experience with the gloom of darkness, with the forces of evil and sin. In our deepest longing—and therefore our prayer—we beseech God to liberate us from it all; for deep down, instinctually, we yearn for the arrival of the Light. Our hearts and minds, plunged as they are in the obscurity of sin and despair, intuitively know that Christ alone is the true Light, "Light from Light" ("*Lumine de Lumine*"), the Light of our souls, the radiant Light of the World. While feeling the anguish in the depths of our own personal nights, the mystery of Christ's birth arrives as a freeing experience for our lives. As we continue the voyage of life, and sometimes traverse some seemingly brutal periods of darkness, we are able now to experience that we are not alone, that our incarnate Lord has come to provide us his own light, himself. This light is a source of consolation, and through it we also receive the gift of his love and peace, the assurance that all shall be well with us until the day we finally gaze on him in his brilliant light for all eternity.

The mystery of Bethlehem touchingly manifests Christ's light as a tiny infant, who, though God himself, is experiencing natural light—the very light he once created—as a human being for the first time. God the Father, in his infinite love and compassion, brought us into the kingdom of his Son, a kingdom where the powers of darkness are overcome by the light of the Savior at the moment of his birth. In Romans 8, Saint Paul tells us that creation was waiting "with eager longing" for the revelation of God—for creation, until then, was "subjected to futility"—and that it was waiting in hope for a Savior that would deliver it from the "bondage to decay." Saint Paul adds that it was "groaning in labor pains," emphasizing the direness of the human condition prior to the arrival of Christ. That glorious first Christmas night, the angels were singing in the heavens and glorifying God, for they knew the rebellion once committed by our first parents against God—a rebellion that kept humanity enslaved to the kingdom of darkness—had finally run its course. The birth of Jesus announced good tidings for the world, for it transferred humanity as a whole from evil's dark shadows to God's own marvelous light. "By the tender mercy of our God, the dawn from on high will break upon us, to give light to those who sit in darkness and in the shadow of death, to guide our feet into the way of peace" (Lk. 1:78–79).

> *At your first coming to us, O Christ,*
> *Your will was to save the children of Adam's race;*
> *When you come again to judge us,*
> *Show mercy to those who honor today*
> *Your holy Nativity in Bethlehem.*
> —Canon for the Prefeast of the Nativity

16.
Jesus of Nazareth

When they had finished everything required by the law of the Lord, they returned to Galilee, to their own town of Nazareth. The child became strong, filled with wisdom; and the favor of God was upon him.
—Luke 2:39–40

Then he went down with them and came to Nazareth, and was obedient to them. His mother treasured all these things in her heart.
—Luke 2:51

There he made his home in a town called Nazareth, so that what had been spoken through the prophets might be fulfilled, "He will be called a Nazarean."
—Matthew 2:23

Then Jesus, knowing all that was to happen to him, came forward and asked them, "Whom are you looking for?" They answered, "Jesus of Nazareth." Jesus replied, "I am he."
—John 18:4–5

The Gospels record little about Jesus's time in Nazareth, but that period of his life is extremely important to his subsequent ministry. Those quiet years in the company of his parents and friends who so deeply loved him were the best preparation for his announcement of the Kingdom of God and the redemptive sacrifice that followed. Jesus made a specific point by beginning his public ministry in Nazareth (see Lk. 4:21).

Jesus's life in Nazareth was one of silence, study, obedience to his parents, prayer, friendship, and work. He concentrated on his spiritual growth, becoming daily more and more attuned to the Father's plan for him, gradually growing "in wisdom and stature, and in favor with God and men" (Lk. 2:52 NASB). He knew that he needed this time of preparation, so as to later accomplish the Father's mission. Even today, from the quiet silence of Nazareth, Jesus reminds each of us to cultivate our own spiritual life, for without it we remain deaf to God's voice and to his plans for us.

In Nazareth Jesus led an ordinary existence of work and filial piety. At times, we are tempted by the idea that in order to please God we must do great things for his glory. We forget the value of the small things which make up our daily lives. A call to do extraordinary things for God is really the exception rather than the rule. To please God, he asks only that we perform the small actions of everyday life in a well-ordered fashion. This is precisely what Jesus did in Nazareth and, thus, this is the mystery and lesson of Nazareth.

One of the most remarkable men of the twentieth century, Charles de Foucauld, in his tender love for his "beloved

Lord Jesus," not only tried to imitate the life of the Savior in Nazareth, but went to live in Nazareth for three years, so as to understand better the Savior's hidden years. While at Nazareth, he wrote about his new understanding of the Lord's early years in his 1930 book, *Meditations of a Hermit*:[4]

My God, you appear in the likeness of man, and becoming man you make yourself the lowest of men. Yours was a life of abjection. You took the lowest of the low places. You went down with them, to live their life, the life of the poor working people, living by their labor. Your life, like theirs, was poor, laborious, hard-working. They were humble and obscure. You lived in the shade of their obscurity. You went to Nazareth, a little village, lost, hidden in the mountains whence, it was said, "no good came forth." . . .

You were subject to them under their authority, as a son is to his father or his brother. It was a life of submission, of filial submission. You were a good obedient son. If your parents' wishes were not in perfect accord with your divine vocation you would not carry them out. You would rather "obey God than man," as when you stayed those three days in Jerusalem. But except in such a case when your vocation would claim you rather than the fulfilling of their wishes, you would fulfill them like the best of sons, not only obeying their smallest wish, but forestalling them, doing all that could give them pleasure, consoling them, making life sweet and pleasant for them, trying, with all your heart, to make them happy, being a model for all sons, having great thought for your parents, that is to say, in the measure allowed you by your vocation. . . .

Thus during those thirty years you were, as a Son, always tender, compassionate, sympathetic, kind. You gave all the happiness you could to your parents, helping, supporting, encouraging them in their daily labor, taking the greater part on yourself to save them fatigue, never crossing them except when the Son of God required it, and then what sweetness and gentleness you would show, so that your nonacquiescence would be sweeter to them than obedience; it would be like a heavenly dew, full of that grace and delicacy and consideration with which a beautiful soul makes life sweet to others. Nothing was left out that could make your parents' life happy and make their little home a heaven.

O Jesus mine,
O Lord divine.
What will you have me give?
Unless You show,
I cannot know,
Nor ever peaceful live.

I give my heart,
And for my part
Beg your Heart in return.
This noble prize

Before my eyes,
All other gifts I spurn.

Do not, O love,
Deprive me of
This prize, my God, but deign
Your heart and mine
As one may shine,
Afire with love's pure flame.
—W. Nakatenus, Cologne, 1903

17.
Jesus in the Jordan: Our Manifested Lord (The Theophany)

Arise! Shine, for your light has come,
the glory of the Lord has dawned upon you.
Though darkness covers the earth,
and thick clouds, the peoples,
Upon you the Lord will dawn,
and over you his glory will be seen.
Nations shall walk by your light,
kings by the radiance of your dawning.
> —Isaiah 60:1–3 (NABRE)

In the power of His gifts John was enabled to baptize,
though earthy, the heavenly.
> —Saint Ephrem the Syrian, Hymn III,
> "On Christ's Nativity"

Each year in early winter, during its darkest and gloomiest of days, we celebrate three liturgical feasts: Christmas, Epiphany, and the Theophany of the Lord, which recall in a special way God's manifestation to all people, to the whole world. On Christmas Day, God's human face became visible to all for the first time in the form of a baby. In the sacred humanity of Christ—God's only begotten Son and the Father's true image and substance—the world was able to behold the splendor, glory, and beauty of God-made-man. Christ's appearance in our midst changed forever the course of human history; this is the mystery of the Incarnation. God manifested himself to our world as a small baby, but he came as Savior—he came to save us all.

The Sunday after Epiphany, we are guided by the angels no longer toward Bethlehem, but to the banks of the Jordan, where another great revelation, a very special manifestation, is awaiting us. When we finally arrive at our destination—the humble waters of the Jordan—without fully knowing what to expect, we witness a glorious manifestation of God's intimate life. During this very special moment as Jesus accepts the baptism of John in the Jordan, the supreme mystery of the Trinity is present and reveals itself for the first time in the New Testament. The one true God is essentially three persons: Father, Son, and Holy Spirit. Already during Compline of the Theophany prefeast, we hear a hymn proclaim:

> *Let streams of tears wash out our eyes,*
> *Let us cleanse our souls from the filth, O believer,*
> *For we shall see Christ,*
> *The light from the threefold light,*
> *Coming to the Jordan to be baptized.*
> *The Father will bear witness from heaven above,*
> *And the Holy Spirit will descend upon him*
> *In the form of a shining dove.*

As we have learned previously, Epiphany and Theophany mean manifestation: God's manifestation to all people, his appearance in the world. Baptism is a symbol of a deeper reality, one that grants us sanctification and total renewal. Through his baptism in the Jordan, Christ comes to sanctify the whole of creation. He comes to redeem and renew wounded, sinful humanity. When Jesus plunges in the depths of the Jordan, all things are made new. His humble reception of water from the hands of John the Baptizer reveals the depth and purpose of his coming into our world.

The early church fathers expressed more beautifully than anyone else the mystical and ontological implications of the Lord's baptism in the Jordan. Saint Justin writes: "When Jesus came to the river Jordan, where John was baptizing, he stepped down into the water and a fire ignited the waters of the Jordan." Saint Ireneus implies that in the precise moment of the Baptism, the Father anoints the entire cosmos. Saint Ireneus also writes that the Father bestows upon the Son the name of Christ "because the Father anointed and adorned all things through him." Saint Paul points to this cosmic dimension: "For in him were created all things in heaven and on earth, the visible and the invisible, whether thrones or dominions or principalities or powers; all things were created through him and for him. He is before all things, and in him all things hold together" (Col. 1:16–17 NABRE). All people, all nations, all worlds and planets, are touched and affected by it.

Saint Ephrem, that humble monk, mystic, and poet from Syria, uses the womb image to express the mystery at hand in the Jordan. Poetically he writes:

The river in which Christ was baptized
conceives him again symbolically:
The moist womb of the water
Conceived him in purity,
bore him in chastity,
made him go up in glory.
In the pure womb of the river
you should recognize Mary
the daughter of Man,
who conceived, having known no man,
who gave birth without intercourse,
who brought up through a gift,
the Lord of that gift.
As the Daystar in the river,
the bright one in the tomb,
He shone forth on the mountaintop
and gave brightness too in the womb;
He dazzled as he went up from the river
and enlightened the world by his ascent.

Saint Ephrem, with a keen mystic sense, associates Christ's baptism and manifestation in the Jordan to the other events and mysteries in Christ's life: his glorious incarnation, dazzling transfiguration, redemptive death, and blessed resurrection and ascension into heaven. With that unique intuition of his, Saint Ephrem links the Jordan event to Pentecost, to our own baptisms, and to the mystery of the Eucharist:

Fire and Spirit are in the womb
of her who bore you, O Christ.
Fire and Spirit are in the river
in which you were baptized.
Fire and Spirit are in our baptism,
and in the bread and cup is fire and the Holy Spirit.

Each year, on the glorious Feast of the Theophany, a feast in which we discover anew a river ablaze in fire, a feast in which the mystery of God is revealed as a communion of three distinct divine Persons, we discover the ever-humbled Christ, our manifested Lord, becoming one like us in all things. Though totally sinless, he enters the waters of the Jordan to identify with our fallen condition and to give us an example of what we must do. He gently invites us to enter into the mystery of our own baptism, a baptism of water and fire, by which we are made and renewed in the image and likeness of God. The Holy Spirit confers new life upon us though the sacraments, and through them he opens wide the doors to God's kingdom.

When in the Jordan, You were baptized, O Lord,
the mystery of the Trinity was made manifest.
For the voice of the Father bore witness to You,
calling You his "Beloved Son."
And the Spirit in the form of a dove
confirmed the truth of these words.
O Christ, our God, who has appeared in the Jordan
to enlighten the world, glory to You.
—Theophany Troparion

18.

Christ's Banquet Hall: Living Manna and Bread from Heaven

Then the LORD *said to Moses, "I am going to rain bread from heaven for you, and each day the people shall go out and gather enough for that day." . . . When the Israelites saw it, they said to one another, "What is it?" . . . Moses said to them, "It is the bread that the* LORD *has given you to eat."*

—Exodus 16:4, 15

Then he took a loaf of bread, and when he had given thanks, he broke it and gave it to them, saying, "This is my body, which is given for you. Do this in remembrance of me." And he did the same with the cup after supper, saying, "This cup that is poured out for you is the new covenant in my blood."

—Luke 22:19–20

Jesus said to them, "Very truly, I tell you, unless you eat the flesh of the Son of Man and drink his blood, you have no life in you. Those who eat my flesh and drink my blood have eternal life, and I will raise them up on the last day; for my flesh is true food and my blood is true drink. Those who eat my flesh and drink my blood abide in me, and I in them."

—John 6:53–56

Every year, on Thursday of Holy Week, we commemorate the mystery of the upper room: the institution of the Eucharist. This is a profound mystery, *mysterium tremendum*, a mystery that lies beyond all possibilities of comprehension, beyond our capacity to understand. As the last days of Jesus's earthly journey begin to wind down, all things converge into those last intimate moments with his disciples, into the Lord's own sacred, last Passover meal. At this mystical supper, Jesus gave the heavenly banquet of his own flesh and blood, a divine gift, to his followers. It is no wonder he says: "I have eagerly desired to eat this Passover with you before I suffer" (Lk. 22:15). He also says, "Where is the guest room, where I may eat this Passover with my disciples?" (Lk. 22:11). During that last meal with his disciples, Jesus leaves for them and all his followers the gift of himself—forever a testament to his boundless and undying love. He loved his disciples, and he loves his followers today, until the very end. As the Gospels tell us, he had no more to give but himself.

During that holy Last Supper, Jesus offered his disciples bread which was broken and wine which was poured—in other words, a life given for them, and blood ready to be poured in sacrifice for their redemption. Each time the Eucharist is reenacted in Jesus's name, he is the offering and sacrificial victim acceptable to the Father, and we are consequently washed and made clean in the blood of the Lamb (see Rev. 7:14).

The only purpose for each Eucharistic celebration is to continue offering the Father a sacrifice of praise. During its reenactment, we the disciples are invited to be fed at the banquet on the body and blood of the Lord. Jesus said, "I am the bread of life," and thus he becomes for us the true bread, "the bread of God . . . which comes down from heaven and gives life to the world" (John 6:33). The Lord, in his love for mankind, provides every one of his disciples easy access to his heavenly banquet. It is the only banquet that promises and provides manna from above. This heavenly manna is a special and precious gift. It strengthens the relationship between Christ—as feeder and food—and us, his unworthy servants partaking of the nourishment. In the holy communion, we are united to Christ and his Father in heaven, and also to all who partake of the same holy meal. As Paul teaches: "The cup of blessing that we bless, is it not a sharing in the blood of Christ? The bread that we break, is it not a sharing in the body of Christ? Because there is one bread, we who are many are one body, for we all partake of the one bread" (1 Cor. 10:16–17).

Speaking of the mystery realized in the Eucharist, Father Matthew the Poor, a renowned Coptic desert monk, writes:

Christ gave us the bread which bears the spirit of eternal life and the mystery of the breaking of his body on the cross. Inevitably, he also gave us the cup of his blood shed for us, in which is the spirit of eternal life. By so doing, he has given us the mystery of total communion with him in his life and his death. Communion here is not metaphorical but actual and factual, confirmed and realized in his words: "He who eats my flesh and drinks my blood abides in me, and I in him" (John 6:56). This mutual abiding means that Christ has a permanent existence in the life of mankind, and this inevitably qualifies for eternal life: "He who eats my flesh and drinks my blood has eternal life, and I will raise him up at the last day" (John 6:54).[5]

Ultimately, we know through faith that the presence of the Lord Jesus in the bread and wine, his holy mysteries, is not only a symbol of our real unity in him, but also an anticipation of the kingdom to come. The presence of the Lord in his mysteries announces his forthcoming arrival in glory at the end of time. Each time we partake of his precious body and blood, we commemorate his death and resurrection, and also announce his final coming, when Christ shall appear and the consummation of our unity with him, the Father, and the Holy Spirit shall be realized and brought to completion for all eternity.

> *Come, O you faithful,*
> *Let us enjoy our Master's hospitality,*
> *The banquet of immortality*
> *In the upper chamber.*
> *With uplifted minds*

Let us receive the divine gifts
From the Word-made-flesh
Whom we magnify.
—The Kanon: Ode 9

19.
Jesus at Mt. Tabor:
The Transfigured Lord

O send out your light and your truth;
let them lead me;
let them bring me to your holy hill
and to your dwelling.

—Psalm 43:3

You have given command to build a temple on your holy
mountain,
and an altar in the city of your habitation,
a copy of the holy tent that you prepared from the
beginning.
With you is wisdom, she who knows your works
and was present when you made the world.

—Wisdom 9:8–9

Now about eight days after these sayings, Jesus took
with him Peter and John and James, and went up on
the mountain to pray. And while he was praying, the
appearance of his face changed, and his clothes became
dazzling white.

—Luke 9:28–29

*The divine Light shone this day on
that blessed mountain.
Mount Tabor is rejoicing, ah rejoicing,
ah rejoicing, rejoicing and exulting!
This day Mount Tabor has flourished
and is filled with luminous flowers.
For Jesus blossomed in the body and
manifested the glory of Adam.*
—Armenian Ode for Transfiguration Day

In the Gospel account of the Transfiguration, we see the explicit desire on the part of the eternal Father to glorify his Son before he undergoes the suffering of his passion. For a moment, the veil covering his divinity is lifted and, suddenly, Jesus appears clothed in unsurpassable beauty. He is luminous, radiant with the Father's glory, to the point of nearly blinding those few who surround him. The disciples present instantly recognize the divine light, the glory of God, shining from his human face. From the mysterious, enveloping cloud, they hear the solemn declaration: "This is my Son, the Beloved; with him I am well pleased; listen to him!" (Matt. 17:5). This is the Father, saying with nearly the exact words he uttered from on high at the moment of Jesus's baptism, the Lord's Theophany, that Jesus is the only Son of God, true God from true God, as we profess and assent in the Credo.

Often, as I read and reread the Transfiguration account in the Gospels, I am led back precisely to that other glorious event, the Lord's Theophany in the Jordan. Both remind us that Christ, the Son of God, never left the Father's side when he descended from heaven to become one of us. In both Transfiguration and Theophany, he unites heaven and earth, the divine and the human. Along with the Incarnation, the birth of the Son of God, the Lord's death on Good Friday, and his glorious resurrection on Easter Sunday, the Transfiguration and Theophany are transcendent cosmic events. They changed the world and the course of history forever.

The mystery of the Lord's Transfiguration is so rich and powerful, so dense with theological thought, that many saints spend their entire lives in its contemplation, trying to deepen, live by, and decipher its message. Certainly, monks of the East such as Saint Ephrem, Saint Gregory Palamas, and Saint Symeon the New Theologian saw a unique cosmic dimension: the transformation of the entire world by Christ's presence in it, the presence of the God-made-man. As one of the Byzantine hymns asserts: "To show the transformation of human nature at your second and fearful coming, O Savior, you did transfigure yourself. And you have sanctified the whole world by your light."

The world at large, which is now under the lure of sin, shall be freed and transformed when the Savior returns in glory at the end of time. The blinding light of Tabor, the light which shone from Jesus's face, sanctified the disciples that come close to him. Today, that same light continues to nurture our best hopes for the future of the cosmos, the world that God created at the beginning of time. The light of the Transfiguration points the path to a new future, a future in which God shall be all in all. Thus and then, we shall utter together eternal praise as we humbly immerse ourselves in the company of Moses and Elijah, of Peter, James, and John. As we witness that mysterious blinding light, the "uncreated light of God," we are moved to praise our transfigured Lord with the words of the Transfiguration sticheras:[6]

Let all the earth be moved to praise Christ, our God,
Lord, both of the living and the dead.
For when he was divinely transfigured on Tabor,
the Savior of our souls was pleased to have at his side
the leaders and preachers of both the Law and Grace.
The shining cloud of the Transfiguration has replaced
the darkness of the Law.
Moses and Elijah were found worthy of this glory
brighter than light
and taken up with it,
and they said unto Christ:
"You are our God, the King of ages."

20.
Christ at Cana: A Unique Relationship with His Mother

On the third day, there was a wedding in Cana of Galilee, and the mother of Jesus was there. Jesus and his disciples had also been invited to the wedding. When the wine gave out, the mother of Jesus said to him, "They have no wine." And Jesus said to her, "Woman, what concern is that to you and to me? My hour has not yet come." His mother said to the servants, "Do whatever he tells you."
—John 2:1–5

Jesus did this, the first of his signs, in Cana of Galilee, and revealed his glory; and his disciples believed in him.
—John 2:11

The LORD is faithful in all his words, and gracious in all his deeds. The LORD upholds all who are falling, and raises up all who are bowed down. The eyes of all look to you, and you give them their food in due season. You open your hand, satisfying the desire of every living thing. The Lord is near to all who call on him, to all who call on him in truth.
—Psalm 145:13–16, 18

The story of the miracle at Cana, as we read it in the Gospel of John, is striking for its directness and beautiful simplicity. The style of the story tells us a great deal about what actually happened there. It is a very refreshing and deeply human story, full of subtle and affectionate nuances in the interplay between a mother and her only son. It is also fascinating to note that, according to John, this event takes place at the onset of the Lord's public life. It is very possible that John was himself present at the wedding, or that he heard the account related firsthand from our Lady's own recollection.

As we enter into the event by reading the account, we become aware of the special circumstances in which the miracle occurs. It is Mary who discovers that there is no more wine at the feast. She feels pity for the newlyweds and for their family and friends. With her typical discretion, she lets her Son know of the embarrassing situation. "They have no wine," she tells Jesus—with all delicacy, but also with full confidence, the type of confidence of which only a mother is capable. She does not force her Son to act, but makes it clear to him that she wishes him to intervene some-how. Mary knows Jesus has no way of providing the needed wine through natural means, but she knows he is the Son of God, with access to extraordinary capabilities. Above all, she trusts in her Son's love for her. She knows he would do anything to please her. The interplay between Mother and Son, and their complete trust and love for one another, is the most beautiful section of the Gospel account—even more beautiful than the miracle itself.

There are so many lessons to learn from the Cana episode. I am always deeply moved while rereading it. One of the great lessons for me is seeing how Jesus responds to his Mother; at her express request he goes out of his way and performs the first recorded miracle of his public life. John makes it very clear: "Jesus did this, the first of his signs, in Cana of Galilee."

Confident in Jesus's love for her, in his compassion for the people at the wedding, and in his extraordinary capacity to help, Mary addresses the servants providing the wine. "Do whatever he tells you." By expecting a divine intervention at the wedding, Mary shows her understanding that Jesus's public mission is beginning, and that this stage in his life will be one in which his supernatural powers will be manifested as proof that he is the Messiah, the Anointed One of God.

Note the importance of Cana for both Jesus and Mary. From reading the Gospel account, one gets the impression that the performance of a miracle at that time was not part of Jesus's plan. This is why he responds to his Mother, "Woman, what concern is that to you and to me?" But, seemingly at his Mother's personal request, Jesus doesn't hesitate to change his plans and hasten the revealing of his divine power. Mary never forgot the words of the angel Gabriel at the moment of the Annunciation: "Nothing is impossible for God" (Lk. 1:37 CEB). Thus with complete and blind faith, she requests what she knows to be possible because her Son is also the very Son of God, capable of performing wonders.

As we move on with our busy day-to-day lives, trying to enter into the mystery of Christ discretely, we must not forget the explicit lesson the Lord provides at Cana. Jesus, by all appearances, changed his own life plans at his Mother's request, and used the occasion at Cana to reveal to his disciples and contemporaries that he was the Savior announced by the prophets, the Savior who came into the world to save each of us. By becoming the savior of an unusual situation at the wedding at Cana, Jesus manifests his glory to us: showing he is indeed our own Savior, the only Savior for the world.

Reading the Cana account over and over again, we begin to realize the significant role that Mary plays in Jesus's plan of salvation. The Theotokos's life, guided by the Holy Spirit, is totally integrated into the life and work of her Son. It is the mission she accepted from the Father at the moment of the Incarnation, a mission she carried out and brought to its ultimate fulfillment when, at the end, she stood by her Son at the foot of the cross. One of the Savior's last acts is to entrust his followers to his Mother: "Woman, behold your son," as if to say, "From now on, they are all your children."

> *She gazes on her Son divine,*
> *In whom both God and man combine;*
> *He whom she cradled with delight*
> *now reigns as King in God-head's light.*
> —Saint Peter Damian, "Aurora Velut"

21.

Jesus at Bethany: His Friendships

"Mary has chosen the better part, which will not be taken away from her."
—Luke 10:42

"Lord, [Lazarus] whom you love is ill."
—John 11:3

"Jesus loved Martha and her sister and Lazarus."
—John 11:5

Bethany brings to mind a topic not often reflected upon, or at least not reflected upon enough: the friendships of Jesus. Anyone who reads the Gospels can certainly see the revered roles the Lord assigned to friendship, human emotion, intimacy, human closeness, and loving others: starting with the real love he had for his parents, Mary and Joseph, and continuing on and on, with the trusting human intimacy he shared with the apostles, the disciples, his particular friends, and close followers. Jesus, the Word of God, become totally human in everything except sin, says Saint Paul. In embracing our lowly humanity, he embraced all the feelings and emotions of which human beings are capable. He embraced human love in its totality, first as fulfillment of the commandment to love your neighbor as yourself, and second, raising it to a most noble and high level, by telling us that there was no greater proof of love than to give one's life for a friend.

In Bethany, we see how comfortable Jesus is in the company of his dear friends, Mary, Martha, and Lazarus, and how comfortable they are with him. Real friendship is always a two-way street. It is very touching that just before undergoing his Passion, one of the last visits Jesus paid was to the home of Mary, Martha, and Lazarus. He went to console these dear friends after the painful loss of their brother Lazarus. Jesus felt the pain so deeply that he cried when he heard that his beloved friend had died. And lo and behold, he goes one step further, doing what only a man who is also God can do: he calls Lazarus forth from the tomb. Can anyone ever doubt the extent and power of Jesus's love? In all instances he is pure, boundless, infinite love. The example of his life, totally motivated and guided by love, should be for us sufficient reason to pursue the work of love at all costs. Love for one another was his message and the only authentic proof of true discipleship. "By this everyone will know that you are my disciples, if you have love for one another" (John 13:35).

Lord Jesus Christ,
While wishing to see the tomb of Lazarus—

for you were soon to dwell in your own tomb by your
own free choice—
You asked: "Where have you laid him?"
And learning that which was already known to You,
You cried out to him whom You have loved:
"Lazarus, come forth."
And he who was without breath
obeyed the One who gave him breath, You, O Lord,
the true Savior of our souls.
                    —Stichera for Lazarus Saturday

22.

Jesus at Golgotha: A Suffering Servant and Crucified Lord

Surely he has borne our infirmities
and carried our diseases;
yet we accounted him stricken,
struck down by God, and afflicted.
But he was wounded for our transgressions,
crushed for our iniquities;
upon him was the punishment
that made us whole,
and by his bruises we are healed.
All we like sheep have gone astray;
we have all turned to our own way,
and the LORD *has laid on him*
the iniquity of us all.

—Isaiah 53:4–6

After this, when Jesus knew that all was now finished,
he said (in order to fulfill the scripture), "I am thirsty."
A jar full of sour wine was standing there. So they put a
sponge full of the wine on a branch of hyssop and held
it to his mouth. When Jesus had received the wine, he

said, "It is finished." Then he bowed his head and gave up his spirit.

—John 19:28–30

True reverence for the Lord's Passion means fixing the eyes of our heart on Jesus Crucified and recognizing in him our own humanity.

—Saint Leo the Great, Sermon on the Passion

Christ's death on the Cross should live in our thoughts and imagination, for frequent thought on the Passion of Christ keeps aflame and brings to intense heat the fires of earnest piety.

—Saint Bonaventure, Holiness of Life

As I turn my thoughts to Jesus's last journey to Golgotha, to Calvary, I try to look back at our yearly experience. Good Friday in a monastery is a day of profound mourning, for we accompany the Savior during his last steps on the way to Calvary. There we witness his drinking and tasting the last drops of the suffering cup, drinking them to the full and to the end. During the Tenebrae Offices, the psalms relate the intensity of Christ's pains, the loneliness of his agony. The Lamentations are usually sung in a grave and sorrowful tone, one that conveys the Lord's heart drowning in a sea of pain. The grievous torments of the crucified Lord echo in our poor, grateful souls, for it is the burden of our iniquities he bears. It is the price of our redemption for which he pays.

We follow each step: the agony and sweating of blood in the garden, the betrayal of Judas, his arrest by the soldiers, the trial before Annas and Caiaphas during the night hours, Peter's fears and betrayal, the court trial before Pontius Pilate, the pillar scourging by the soldiers, the carrying of a heavy cross and the encounter with his Mother on the way to Calvary, and, lastly, the cruel death and burial. Deeply moved, we fall down in wonder and adoration before our crucified Lord, praying, singing, lamenting, and repeating over and over again the Byzantine antiphon: "Glory to your Passion, O Christ. Glory to your long-suffering, O Lord." And as we sing, we usually alternate with other Byzantine texts, always as poignant: "Adore your Bridegroom covered with blood, and in your kiss give him your entire self." And again: "Before your Cross, we bow down in worship, O Master, and your Holy Resurrection we glorify."

Every year in the monastery, as the Passion accounts of Holy Week are read over and over, we learn anew how Christ fulfilled perfectly the role of the suffering servant, promised centuries before by the prophet Isaiah. The Gospels have many stories that link Jesus's passion directly to Isaiah's prophecies. Most striking is the passage in Isaiah that indicates the type of torment, pain, and death the suffering servant would endure in the last days of his life. In accomplishing the mission assigned to him by the Father, Christ, God's servant, would know nothing but extreme and excruciating suffering. But Isaiah also promises that God will always be with his Son, even if at times it may not seem so; he will help and vindicate him, and in the end he will glorify him. It is obvious that Isaiah's account of the suffering servant points directly to Jesus of Nazareth, the Son of Man. Furthermore, several of the Evangelists state clearly in the Gospels that the suffering servant role is fulfilled in Jesus.

During the time of Jesus, death by crucifixion was a typical Roman technique for punishing someone who received a death sentence. They used this method especially for those who opposed or questioned their mighty political power. When Jesus is finally sentenced by Pilate, attached to the sentence is the cruel provision that he must carry his own cross. At one point, a bystander, Simon of Cyrene, is asked to help Jesus carry the cross. On that painful journey to Golgotha, a crowd of people follow; the Lord's final hours are made into a spectacle to entertain the crowds. Some of Jesus's own followers, especially the women, bewail and lament their master's torments. Jesus responds to their compassion and tells them, "Daughters of Jerusalem, do not weep for me, but weep for yourselves and your children."

When Jesus, the soldiers, and the crowd arrive at Golgotha, the Lord is offered sour wine mixed with myrrh. He tastes it, but refuses to drink. It was a custom among the Romans to offer a drink to someone condemned. They pretended it alleviated the prisoner's sensitivity to severe pain, especially at the time of crucifixion. Everyone present knew the immense pain and suffering brought about by crucifixion. It was totally unbearable. According to the Gospels, Christ's crucifixion takes place at the third hour, around 9:00 A.M. The Lord is fastened to the cross with huge nails. After the cross is lifted up, Jesus pronounces a few words quietly, painfully. Seven of his sentences are recorded in the Gospels. The first sentence is: "Father, forgive them, for they know not what they are doing" (Lk. 23:34). While in the midst of utter desolation, Jesus prays for those responsible for his sufferings: the mean crowds; the members of the Sanhedrin; Pilate and the Roman soldiers who crucified him; and, lastly, for all of us.

In spite of his prayers and forgiveness, the soldiers and the crowd continue their mockery: "He saved others; he cannot save himself" (Matt. 27:42). One of the criminals next to him asks Jesus to remember him when the Lord reaches his kingdom. Jesus replies, "Truly I tell you, today you will be with me in Paradise" (Lk. 23:43). As he is undergoing the cruelest of tortures, Jesus doesn't hesitate to show compassion to anyone asking for it. At that instance, he makes a promise to his criminal neighbor. He promises him the blessedness of eternal life.

Around the ninth hour, 3:00 PM, feeling his final hour arriving and undergoing extreme pain and suffering, desperate and abandoned, he utters the words: "My God, my God, why have you forsaken me?" (Ps. 22:1). Who could ever imagine the depths of his sufferings, physically, psychologically, spiritually, emotionally? He had to endure it all to save each of us, the fallen. Before giving up his last breath, Jesus utters his final words: "Father, into your hands I commend my spirit." At the very end, with total filial submission, Jesus entrusts himself to his Father. His death is a voluntary act of submission, of total obedience to his Father.

And as he gets ready to depart, he exclaims his famous, "*Consumatum est*"—"It is all finished." His mission is completed. He always spoke of "his hour," and now that hour has arrived. His work has been accomplished on the wood of a tree, the wood of the cross. At the same time, the hour for his glorification has also arrived. At the very moment of his death on the cross—at that boundless instant—Christ destroyed sin and overcame the power of eternal death. By his death on a cross, Jesus manifested to the world the power of God, the divine power that offers new life to humanity and the promise of an eternal resurrection. It was only then, after Jesus died and the temple curtain was torn in two, that one of the nearby soldiers exclaimed: "Indeed this man was the son of God" (Mk. 15:39 DRA).

The mystery of Christ's death on the cross, of his ultimate *kenosis* (self-emptying) and Passover, lies in the fact that Christ was not liable to the punishment of death as we are. In his love for his Father, Christ deliberately chose and accepted death to redeem a world wounded by sin. It is only through the passion and death of Christ, therefore, that we humans can overcome the slavery brought by sin and death and reach God's kingdom of life and grace. As Edith Stein, in all her wisdom, used to remind others, "Only the Passion of Christ can save us."

> *O sweetest Christ, what did you do*
> *that You should be treated as such?*
> *O, most lovable of youths, what was your sin*
> *that Your judgment should be so severe?*
> *Alas, I am the cause of your grief,*
> *I inflicted You the deadly blow.*
> —Saint Anselm, A Prayer

23.
Jesus at Calvary:
The Mystery of the Cross

Your Cross, O Lord, is life and resurrection to your
  people;
and putting all our trust in it, we sing to You, our cruci-
  fied God:
Have mercy upon us.
> —Byzantine Chant, Service of the 12 Gospels

O tree that shines with beauty rare,
ennobled by Christ's precious Blood,
He chose you as the royal bed
to rest his sacred limbs in death.
> —V. Fortunatus, "Vexilla Regis"

Let us, the faithful, praise and worship the Word, co-
eternal with the Father and the Spirit, born for our
salvation from the Virgin; for He willed to be lifted up
on the Cross in the flesh, to endure death, and to raise
the dead by His glorious Resurrection.
> —Sunday Troparion, Tone 5

The limitless power of God dwells in the cross, just as it resided in an incomprehensible way in the ark which was venerated amidst great honor and awe by the Jewish people, performing miracles and awesome signs in the midst of those who were not ashamed to call it "God," that is, they would gaze upon it in awe as though upon God, because of the glory of God's honored name which was upon it.

—Saint Isaac the Syrian

From its inception, Christianity has kept a continual, sacred remembrance of the mysteries of the suffering, crucifixion, and resurrection of the Lord at its core. Salvation and the new life that Christ offers to the world originate there. This new faith, therefore, required a sacred, visible symbol that could speak to many and to all of the eternal redemption accomplished by Christ. The cross rapidly became that symbol. The cross automatically communicates to the believer the message of Christ's enduring love. Jesus died on the cross for only one purpose: to reconcile us to the Father. The theme of the cross appears frequently in the Christian liturgy, especially in that of the East where the cross is commemorated not only on Good Friday but also on the third Sunday of Lent and on September 14, the Feast of the Exaltation of the Glorious Cross.

Christian theology and tradition inculcates in believers a sincere veneration for the Cross. We know for certain that the True Cross was once washed with the Lord's sacred blood. The Cross served as royal bed to the Lord's body, even if a cruel one, as the Liturgy reminds us in the hymn "Vexilla Regis." As Jesus was crucified and died, the Cross was one with him and he was one with it. Ever since that momentous occasion, all other crosses and crucifixes, images of the first one, are venerated and treated with upmost respect and reverence, for indeed they represent him, Christ, the Author of our salvation. On the Liturgy of Good Friday, as we venerate the cross repeatedly, we sing: "We adore You, O Christ, and we bless You: for by Your holy cross You have redeemed the world."

The cross conveys the mystery of the passion and death of Christ like nothing else. It becomes a divine manifestation through which we have access to the sacrifice of the crucified body of the Lord. On the cross, the heart of Jesus overflowed with love. We pay homage daily to Christ's glorious cross on which our Savior acted out the mystery of our salvation. On the day of our baptism, the cross of Christ was traced over our heads as a seal, marking that from that day forward our lives belong to Christ. As we move on with our lives, making the sign of the cross often and carrying our own little crosses, we embrace the One who gave his own life to save us. On the third Sunday of Lent, the Sunday of the Cross, the Eastern church honors its mystery with these prayerful verses:

> O Lord, *who willingly ascended the cross,*
> *enable us to venerate it with true compunction of heart.*
> *And enlighten us, by the discipline of prayer, fasting,*
> *and good works,*
> *for you are good and love mankind.*

O Lord, cleanse me from my many sins
by the grace of your great mercy.
And enable me to see and kiss Your cross,
on this present week of the great Fast (Lent),
for You are the Lover of mankind.
O wonder of wonders!
The wood on which Christ was voluntarily crucified in
  the flesh
is today venerated and exalted!
The entire world bows down and sings:
"O marvelous might of the cross, I exalt you.
O most precious wood, I honor you and bow down
in reverence and fear,
and glorify God, who through you, granted me life
  eternal."

24.
Jesus of Jerusalem: Our Risen Lord

Why do you look for the living among the dead? He is not here, but has risen. Remember how he told you, while he was still in Galilee, that the Son of Man must be handed over to sinners, and be crucified, and on the third day rise again.

—Luke 24:5–7

This Jesus God raised up, and of that all of us are witnesses. Therefore let the entire house of Israel know with certainty that God has made him both Lord and Messiah, this Jesus whom you crucified.

—Acts 2:32, 36

Christ is Risen from the dead! By death He conquered death, and upon those in the tombs bestowing life.

—Paschal Troparion

Christ is risen and death is overcome. Christ is risen and the devil is crushed. Christ is risen and the angels rejoice. Christ is risen and there are no dead left in the tombs.

Christ rising from the dead has become the first fruits of those that sleep. To him be glory and power throughout the ages. Amen.

—Saint John Chrysostom, A Paschal Homily

In unison with Saint Paul, our faith affirms: "If you confess with your lips that Jesus is Lord and believe in your heart that God raised him from the dead, you will be saved" (Rom. 10:9). None of us can proclaim or even fully understand the mystery of Christ's resurrection, however, without the context of his undergoing the pain and agony of death on a cross first.

In those days after his death, as Jesus lay in the tomb and descended into hell, the victory he achieved on the cross was not visible to his followers. The apostles were still waiting for a sign that Christ's act of redemption had been accepted. It was Christ's glorious resurrection that made manifest his triumph over sin and death. The resurrection of Christ completed his work on earth, the very purpose for which he became man. In the mystery of Jesus's resurrection, we his followers find a new purpose and model for a renewed life of grace and intimacy with God. For we are now truly his accepted and beloved children, totally "alive to God in Christ Jesus" (Rom. 6:11).

Christ's triumph over the powers of darkness means that a new truth has entered our world, something which positively affects our ordinary everyday lives. If we, as Saint Paul counsels us in his letter to the Colossians, set our hearts on things that are above, we shall discover a new life open to the spiritual powers that come from above: we will see everything in a new way, as the risen Christ sees it. Our capacity for this new reality depends on us entirely. God himself sets no limit on the fullness of life and love with which he would endow us. Jesus, by his death and resurrection, has opened this new pathway to truth and love. It is meant for all, and it is open to all of good will who drink from the fountain of immortality that flows from the wounds of the risen Savior. In him, we are invited to partake of this new Passover banquet where eternal life is being offered—where we celebrate the "Feast of Feasts," as the early Fathers called the Easter Pasch, with the "unleavened bread of sincerity and truth."

The resurrection of the Lord provides the believer the occasion to celebrate life, for we now know that death has been conquered and that life exists beyond the grave. Every time we profess our faith in Christ's divine resurrection, we say life is indestructible; we say it is everlasting. This is the good news of Christ's resurrection. Often during the Easter season, while gazing during our Offices at the paschal candle, one seems to experience almost in a palpable manner the mysterious and joyous presence of the risen Lord. The flame from the candle seems to glow brightly in our dark chapel, and that light conveys with certainty something totally undefined but true: a real, mysterious presence in our midst, that of the risen Lord.

One of the most inspiring liturgical texts we sing throughout Easter week, what is called here "Bright Week," is the hymn to the Resurrection composed by Saint John Damascene. The author, like few others, communicates to the believer the profound meaning of the Resurrection event:

Today is the day of the Resurrection!
O nations be illumined.
It is the Passover of the Lord,
In which Christ passed from death to life,
From earth to heaven,
As we sing the song of victory and triumph.

Let us purify our senses
That we may behold Christ shining as lightning
In the splendor of his Resurrection,
Hearing him say to us: Rejoice!
As we sing the song of victory and triumph.

Come, let us drink a new water,
Now drawn from a barren rock,
A new vintage from the fountain of incorruption
That springs from the tomb of Christ,
In Whom we are firmly established.
Let us rise early in the morning,
At the break of dawn
And instead of fragrant ointment
Let us offer pure praise to the Master.
Let us behold Christ, the Sun of Justice,
Giving life and shining upon all.

25.

Jesus of the Mount of Olives:
Our Ascended Lord

*Then he led them out as far as Bethany, and lifting up
his hands, he blessed them. While he was blessing them,
he withdrew from them and was carried up into heaven.*
—Luke 24:50–51

*Do not let your hearts be troubled, and do not let them
be afraid. You heard me say to you, "I am going away
and I am coming to you." If you loved me, you would
rejoice that I am going to the Father, because the Father
is greater than I. And now I have told you this before it
occurs, so that when it does occur, you may believe.*
—John 14:27–29

*O Christ, splendor and glory of the Father,
as we behold your Ascension on the holy mountain,
we sing a hymn to the beauty of your countenance.
We bow down to your Sacred Passion,
we venerate your Resurrection
and glorify your noble Ascension.
O Lord, ascended into glory, have mercy on us.*
—Byzantine Vespers of the Ascension

The Ascension of the Lord is a unique mystery among all the other mysteries in the life of Christ. It is full of majesty, nobility, and at the same time a certain nostalgia, because from now on the physical presence of the Lord is being taken away from human sight. The Ascension, which took place on the Mount of Olives, is all about the final glorification of our gracious Lord and master. Having accomplished his task on earth, Jesus returns to the Father's side, where he is forever exalted in glory, rewarded abundantly for what he endured for our sake. Jesus fulfilled all of the Father's plans, and now returns to his eternal bosom. The Creed would describe him as now being seated forever at the Father's right hand "to judge the living and the dead." Christ is the only true and final judge for all of humanity. Thankfully, he is also our Savior and a merciful one, and trusting in that, we can move forward with our earthly lives, knowing he will judge us according to his great mercy.

In chapter 1 of the book of Acts, its author describes the Ascension scene in this fashion: "When he had said this, as they were watching, he was lifted up, and a cloud took him out of their sight. While he was going and they were gazing up toward heaven, suddenly two men in white robes stood by them. They said, 'Men of Galilee, why do you stand looking up toward heaven? This Jesus, who has been taken up from you into heaven, will come in the same way as you saw him go into heaven'" (Acts 1:9–11). It is interesting to read this rendition of the event, for the liturgical traditions of both the East and the West, while remaining faithful to the biblical account, interpret it in different manners. In the

Eastern church, the Ascension event is described by a Greek word that translates as "the taking up" or "lifted up."

This expression signifies that Jesus, by ascending into his glory, completed his work on earth. In contrast to this, the expression used in the Western church is that of ascension, a gradual elevation, which implies the Lord was raised up to the glory and throne of his Father by his own power. I think both expressions, though different, complement each other and enrich our understanding of the mystery of the Ascension.

The Feast of the Ascension is one of great antiquity. Like most feasts of the Lord, it originated in the East. It was in the Holy Land, the Christian Orient, that the Ascension became a living memory and a permanent tradition among the Lord's disciples. Later on, the church fathers of the East and the West testified through their beautiful homilies and commentaries to the prominence of the mystery of the Ascension from the early life of the church. We, as Christians, can gather a great deal of comfort and strength from meditating often on this particular mystery, the summit and conclusion of Christ's work on earth. We can find comfort and hope in knowing that our Savior, having achieved the end of his earthly pilgrimage, is waiting with open arms to welcome us also into his Father's kingdom. Before departing, he promised to his disciples—that is, to all of us—"I am going to prepare a place for you . . . so that where I am you also may be" (John 14:2–3 NABRE).

*The Lord ascended into heaven to send the Comforter
 into the world.*
*The heavens prepared his throne, the angels marveled
 at his sight.*
*Today the Father receives in his bosom him who was
 always with him.*
*The Holy Spirit commands the angels: "Lift up your
 gates, O you Princes."*
O you nations of the earth, clap your hands,
*for Christ has ascended to the place where he was before
 time begun.*
O Lord, life-giving Christ,
when the apostles saw you ascending upon the clouds,
a great sadness filled them.
They shed burning tears and exclaimed:
O dear Master, do not leave us orphans!
We are your servants whom you love so tenderly.
*As you promised, send your Holy Spirit to enlighten our
 souls.*

—Sticheras, Vespers of the Ascension

PART III

CHRIST
in the Byzantine Tradition

26.

Christ, Savior and Judge

She will bear a son, and you are to name him Jesus, for he will save his people from their sins.
—Matthew 1:21

To you is born this day in the city of David a Savior, who is the Messiah, the Lord.
—Luke 2:11

The Father judges no one but has given all judgment to the Son, so that all may honor the Son just as they honor the Father. Anyone who does not honor the Son does not honor the Father who sent him. Very truly, I tell you, anyone who hears my word and believes him who sent me has eternal life, and does not come under judgment, but has passed from death to life.
—John 5:22–24

Christ, our judge, commands us to be vigilant. We wait expectantly for his holy visitation.
—Compline Prefeast of the Nativity

The Gospel according to Saint Matthew assigns various titles to the Lord: "Messiah," "Savior," "Son of God," and "Emmanuel," among others. In the eyes of the Evangelist narrator, they clearly delineate specific roles Jesus is to fill during his earthly life. By his human descent from David's lineage and divine conception of the Holy Spirit, Jesus is recognized as the Messiah and Son of God the Most High. With the title "Savior," Saint Matthew is reminding us that this tiny child shall one day deliver the people of Israel—all people, really—from the darkness of sin. By using the name Emmanuel, "God with us," he assures us once more that God, according to his promise, shall abide and remain always with his people.

God the Father, in his immense desire to save the world which he created, enters the reality of time. In Christ, our Savior, the Father pours out his infinite love for humankind. In Christ, his Son, he reconciles the world to himself.

The mystery of salvation is closely tied to the mystery of the ultimate judgment. They are inseparable. Christ is assigned both roles—Savior and Judge—by the Father. Our faith tells us that both titles are real, and somehow even surpass reality. Christ is the Judge of evil; and at the same time, he is our Savior and the Lover of mankind, as the Byzantine liturgy often reminds us. We live under the fear of just judgment because of our sins, while at the same time, a blessed hope and trust permeates our life, because we know that he who is to be our Judge is also our Savior: Christ, the all-merciful one.

During our lifetime, we must plunge ourselves humbly into the work of praying assiduously while always loving, hoping, repenting, and being vigilant. We must keep always in mind that in the final confrontation, we shall face the Judge-Savior who gave even the last drop of his own blood to save us. "In you, O Lord, I have placed my hope. Don't let me be confounded forever."

Hear my prayer, O LORD;
give ear to my supplications in your faithfulness;
answer me in your righteousness.
Do not enter into judgment with your servant,
for no one living is righteous before you.

Save me, O LORD, from my enemies;
I have fled to you for refuge.
Teach me to do your will,
for you are my God.
   —Psalm 143:1–2, 9–10

27.
Christ, the Light That Never Sets

Light of the Father,
Jesus Christ our Savior,
Light of your creature,
Showing us the Father,
May we be with you
In the light of heaven
Singing your praises.
   —"Quod Chorus," hymn by Rabanus Maurus, AD 856

Lord of light, shine in our senses,
Scatter the phantoms of our mind.
Our voices sing to You this day,
Offering up our prayers and adoration.
     —Saint Ambrose of Milan, fourth century

Again Jesus spoke to them, saying, "I am the light of the
world. Whoever follows me will never walk in darkness
but will have the light of life."
       —John 8:12

For with You is the fountain of life; in Your light we see light.
       —Psalm 36:9 (NASB)

The Gospel according to John is very revealing when it comes to asserting that Christ, and he alone, is the true light in our otherwise dark world. It points directly to the person of Christ as the source of light. This light is not simply a splendid radiance that shines from his person. It is much, much more, for Christ not only offers light to his followers, but gives himself as light to them. Jesus explains this explicitly: "The light [referring to himself] is with you for a little longer. Walk while you have the light, so that the darkness [the enemy] may not overtake you. If you walk in the darkness, you do not know where you are going. While you have the light, believe in the light, so that you may become children of light" (John 12:35–36). We can only become a disciple of Jesus, a follower, by accepting totally the light he offers us: himself. Jesus is both light and life; thus we are doubly enriched by the gift of himself.

In his homily for the beautiful Feast of the Presentation of the Lord in the Temple, the Hypapante—a festival of lights par excellence—the seventh-century bishop Saint Sophronius describes the role of Christ as light, a true light to our own souls and a light for the whole world:

The Mother of God, the most pure Virgin, carried the true light in her arms and brought Him to those who were sitting in darkness. We too, my children, must carry a light for everyone to see and ponder the shining radiance of the true light as we hasten to meet the Lord. Truly, the Light has come and has shone upon a world enveloped in shadows, the Orient from on high has visited us and given light to those sitting in darkness. This, then, is our festival, and with lighted candles we join in the procession to reveal the light that has shone upon us and the glory that is yet to arrive to us through him. So let us all hasten together to meet our Lord and God.

Our true light has shined and it has come, the light that enlightens everyone who is born into this world. Let all of us, therefore, be enlightened and made radiant by this light. Let us all share into its splendor and glory, and be so filled with it that there no longer remains room for darkness. Let us shine ourselves as we move forward to meet with the elder Simeon in the light whose glow is eternal. Rejoicing with Simeon and Anna, let us sing a thanksgiving hymn to God, the Father of the Light, who sent the true light to dispel our darkness and to give us all a partaking of His eternal splendor.

Christ reminds each of us Christians that he alone is the Light of the World, the "uncreated light," the true sun that never sets; it is up to us, therefore, to live and to walk in that light—that is, in Christ. To live in Christ and with Christ is to abide permanently in the reality of his light, of his love, and of his life. Love, light, and life are all interrelated and true signs that we are sincere, honest disciples of a master. Our lives must shine with the radiant light of Jesus. As Saint Paul in his Letter to the Ephesians reminds us: "Once you were in darkness, but now in the Lord you are light. Live as children of light—for the fruit of the light is found in all that is good and right and true" (Eph. 5:8–9).

O Christ-God, our endless Light,
the Most High, the Unapproachable;
you are the God that cannot be conceived by the mind
or spoken by the lips.
You are the Light and Life-Giver for every rational
  creature.
As our God, you are to the world of spiritual intellect,
what the sun is to the sensory world.
And your Light manifests divinity to our minds
to the degree that we are purified and ready for it.

28.
Christ the Bridegroom

For as a young man marries a young woman, so shall your builder marry you, and as the bridegroom rejoices over the bride, so shall your God rejoice over you.
—Isaiah 62:5

Now John's disciples and the Pharisees were fasting, and people came and said to him, "Why do John's disciples and the disciples of the Pharisees fast, but your disciples do not fast?" Jesus said to them, "The wedding guests cannot fast while the bridegroom is with them, can they? As long as they have the bridegroom with them, they cannot fast. The days will come when the bridegroom is taken away from them, and then they will fast on that day."
—Mark 2:18–20

Look! Here is the bridegroom! Come out to meet him.
—Matthew 25:6

Heralds proclaim the Bridegroom's invitation. All mankind is called to the wedding feast, for He is a generous

lover. Once the crowd has assembled, the Bridegroom
decides who will enter the wedding feast.
    —Saint Cyril of Jerusalem

To comprehend in depth the rich symbolism of Christ as the true Bridegroom—the Lover of mankind, as he is called in the Byzantine tradition—we need to believe and accept that our God is a jealous God, one who cannot tolerate sharing his bride—each one of us—with any other earthly lover. Christ, the Bridegroom, is mystically united to his bride, the church, for he shed his own blood as the price for its redemption. The Church—that is, all of us—is therefore permanently united to the mystical Bridegroom by a debt of perpetual gratitude for his gift of salvation.

The Bridegroom seals the intimate relationship that he has with each of us, his members, through the sacraments, especially the Eucharist, by which he consummates his complete union and oneness with each of us. The Eucharist is the marriage feast of the Lamb as described in the book of Revelation, and through it we experience a rare and unique union with the Bridegroom. It is a union that on one level includes all other members of his body, our brothers and sisters in the faith, and on another level includes his divine family—that is, the Father and the Holy Spirit. Before departing from this world, the Bridegroom made these promises to his disciples: "If you love me, you will keep my commandments. And I will ask the Father, and he will give you another Advocate, to be with you forever. This is the Spirit of truth" (John 14:15–17). He added, "Those who love me will keep my word, and my Father will love them, and we will come to them and make our home with them" (John 14:23).

Throughout the year, I partake daily in the grace of praying and venerating the austere Bridegroom icon that our friend and neighbor Olga painted for our chapel a few years ago. This encounter with the icon becomes more and more intense, more intimate, during the whole of the Lenten journey, particularly during the first three days of Holy Week, when we pray and sing and weep during the long hours of the Bridegroom Offices. The icon is also a special and helpful presence in times of anguish, sickness, and distress. The icon firmly reminds me that all that matters is Christ, and he alone. Daily we live and die with him. The Bridegroom in the icon inspires love and forgiveness. He also inspires acceptance, compassion, and great trust. Through my tender repetition of the Jesus Prayer, the Lord allows me to enter into the icon and remain there with him. While there, a profound realization grows in me, and I become mindful of only one thing: it is the blessed Bridegroom's company that our souls hunger for. We can never get any satisfaction except when prostrated in his silent presence. If the Bridegroom wasn't there, we would certainly perish. But he is there, and our hands hold fast unto his cloak and we pray to never let go of it.

Churches and monasteries in the Byzantine tradition celebrate the Bridegroom Offices as the required preparation for Holy Thursday, Good Friday, and Holy Saturday. The icon of the Bridegroom is solemnly enthroned in the center aisle of the church, and the mournful singing begins, reminding us of the trial and death of the Lord, of his patient endurance throughout. In the ritual and lamenting words of the service, we relive the long hours of Christ's agony—every moment of his sacred passion—as we seek to accompany him to the very end at Calvary. These are the sufferings not of an ordinary man, but of the God-man, in whose person the divine and human natures coexist. The stanzas of the Bridegroom hymns are so expressive and beautiful, especially when prayerfully sung:

> *Behold, the Bridegroom arrives in the middle of the*
> *   night.*
> *Happy is that servant whom he shall find watching.*
> *On the contrary, unworthy is he who is careless and not*
> *   ready.*
> *Let us, then, be vigilant and put aside the works of*
> *   darkness,*
> *Lest we fall into deep slumber,*
> *For the Lord shall arrive as a thief in the night.*

> *O Bridegroom, more beautiful than all men.*
> *Having called us to the spiritual feast of Your kingdom,*
> *Now clothe us with the right wedding garment.*
> *That being adorned in the garment of your beauty,*
> *We may enter into your bridal chamber as your guests*
> *Shining with glory and joy.*

Let us cast aside the works of darkness
And go out to meet Christ, the immortal Bridegroom,
Carrying sufficient oil in the vessels of our souls,
Strengthened by prayer and fasting.
Vigilantly let us await the Bridegroom, arriving near
For the bridal chamber is ready,
And the wedding feast is at hand.
Let us love the Bridegroom
By readying our lamps, shining with virtues and deep
  faith,
That like the wise virgins of the Lord well prepared,
We may enter with Christ into the wedding feast
And receive from the Bridegroom the wedding garment,
So that God may grant us an incorruptible crown.

29.

Christ the Pantokrator:
His Power and Majesty

O LORD, our Sovereign,
how majestic is your name in all the earth!
You have set your glory above the heavens.
    —Psalm 8:1

And Jesus came and said to them, "All authority in
heaven and on earth has been given to me."
    —Matthew 28:18

We did not follow cleverly devised myths when we made
known to you the power and coming of our Lord Jesus
Christ, but we have been eyewitnesses of his majesty. For
he received honor and glory from God the Father when
that voice was conveyed to him by the Majestic Glory,
saying, "This is my Son, my Beloved, with whom I am
well pleased." We ourselves heard this voice come from
heaven, while we were with him on the holy mountain.
    —2 Peter 1:16–18

Bless the LORD, O my soul.
O LORD my God, you are very great.
You are clothed with honor and majesty,
wrapped in light as with a garment.
　　　　　　　　—Psalm 104:1–2

The chapel, our humble monastic oratory, is built facing east, as were most early monastic churches. Monks were always attentive to the Lord's words: "For as the lightning comes from the east and flashes as far as the west, so will be the coming of the Son of Man" (Matt. 24:27). It makes perfect sense to continue preserving the ancient, venerable, and holy custom of praying toward the east. A life-size icon of Christ the Pantokrator, enthroned in majesty, is at the very center in the apse of our chapel, toward which we raise our prayer daily. At the Lord's sides are icons of the Theotokos, the Holy Mother, and the Precursor, John the Baptist. Both of them, with hands pointing directly to the Lord, make quiet and fervent intercession for us. In Greek the trio of icons together are called the *Deesis*, which means "intercession." Christ looks with a certain gravity at us, while his Mother, the Theotokos, and John the Forerunner silently plead our cause.

The Pantokrator is an old Greek title given to our Lord and Savior from ancient times. When the Scriptures were first translated from Hebrew into Greek, the Old Testament translators used the word *pantokrator* to convey what the Hebrews called *El Shaddai*, which meant "Almighty" or "All-Powerful." This Greek expression is interpreted as omnipotence, the ability to do anything. Another translation of the Greek work is "ruler of all" or "sustainer of the world." All these translations portray the immensity of God's mighty power, the fact that God is capable of accomplishing everything.

Monks here in this small monastery, as well as most Orthodox, prefer to call the Lord by the title Pantokrator in contrast to titles such as Ruler or All-Powerful because the name goes further to convey the idea that God, in Christ, is intimately involved in the processes of the world. He holds everything together by his constant, loving care. He is, himself, love.

The concept and image of Christ the Pantokrator stretches beyond the concept of God in the Old Testament, where the ancient Israelites saw mostly God as the Creator and the giver of the law. With the arrival of the Son of God into our world, we were given a new way of contemplating God's mystery. The majestic icon of the Pantokrator conveys both the idea of the all-powerful and all-knowing God as he was seen in the Old Testament and the human-incarnate image of Christ-God, who became flesh for our sake and now appears and is perceived as one of us. Thus, the Pantokrator icon, in all its mysterious majesty and glory, becomes the visible and human image of the invisible God.

Saint Paul, in his Letter to the Colossians, describes better than anyone what the mystery and title of Christ the Pantokrator signifies: "He is the image of the invisible God, the firstborn of all creation; for in him all things in heaven and on earth were created, things visible and invisible, whether thrones or dominions or rulers or powers—all things have been created through him and for him. He himself is before all things, and in him all things hold together. For in him all the fullness of God was pleased to dwell, and through him God was pleased to reconcile to himself all things" (Col. 1:15–17, 19–20). The Pantokrator's image is beautifully portrayed in Byzantine icons, frescoes, and mosaics.

The title appears eight or nine times in the original Greek of the book of Revelation. It is first registered in Revelation when the Lord is quoted as saying: "I am the Alpha and the Omega . . . who is and who was and who is to come" (Rev. 1:8 NABRE). He, the Pantokrator, is then understood to be truly almighty God, the God of creation, the law, and the burning bush, the God who once said to Moses, "I AM who AM." He is also now Emmanuel, the God of the Incarnation, Crucifixion, and Resurrection. He is always with us, seated at the right hand of the Father, making intercession for us, and promises to remain there beyond the end of time. As we ponder in awe the glory and majesty of the Son of God, Christ the Pantokrator, we can humbly say with the psalmist, "How wonderful is your name, Lord, God of hosts."

> *O Christ, the Ruler of all time,*
> *You hold the world beneath your sway,*
> *As Judge supreme of every soul*
> *We offer You our hearts this day.*
> *O Christ, our Shepherd, Prince of Peace,*
> *Our rebel hearts and minds subdue,*
> *And draw the sheep that roam astray,*
> *Within the fold, at one with You.*
> —From the hymn "Te saeculorum"

30.

Christt the Merciful

Have mercy on me, O God,
according to your steadfast love;
according to your abundant mercy
blot out my transgressions.
Wash me thoroughly from my iniquity,
and cleanse me from my sin.
Against you, you alone, have I sinned
and done what is evil in your sight.
     —Psalm 51:1–2, 4a

Lord Jesus Christ, Son of the living God, have mercy on
me, a sinner.

     —Jesus Prayer

There is a special icon of Christ that hangs in a Byzantine museum in Berlin; it is particularly striking, very dear and personal to me. This icon, done in mosaic style, is of rare and extraordinary beauty. There is a gravity and majesty to the Lord's portrayal, so much so that when you glance at the icon, it moves and compels you to prayer. It seems to have originated somewhere in the Mediterranean area, perhaps in the vicinity of Constantinople. Not much is known about it, except an inscription on the side of the image, which clearly states the name given to it: Christ the Merciful.

Many, many years ago—about forty or so—I encountered this icon for the first time, and was totally taken with it immediately. I couldn't let go of its image in my mind. One day I finally managed to get a large print of the icon and carefully mounted it onto a piece of wood specially cut to fit it. It was the closest thing I could have to a real hand-painted copy of the icon. Christ the Merciful nurtured my prayer daily, so much so that the icon became a true resting place for my soul. I was very comfortable in its presence, and if by chance I was away from it for a while, I felt distracted and lost. To remedy this, I acquired a small postcard of the image, which to this day I carry in my French breviary. Both the card and breviary are well worn from their daily use. I never told anyone of my particular closeness and preference for the icon of Christ the Merciful. No one knew how much I treasured it.

As the years passed, a small hermitage was built on our monastery property, at the request of the Little Sisters and Little Brothers of Charles de Foucauld, who for thirty years used it weekly, mostly on weekends and sometimes for retreats lasting forty days or so. When the hermitage was built, a corner of it was made into a small oratory where the sisters and brothers could pray. When the hermitage was inaugurated, I was given the opportunity to choose two permanent icons for the oratory: one of the Lord and another of his Holy Mother, the Theotokos. This was not a difficult choice, and I knew immediately which ones I would opt for: Christ the Merciful and Our Lady of Korsum. I had an identical copy of our Lady's icon in our monastic cell, so fortunately I did not have to part with it. The icon of Christ the Merciful was a different story. It was the only one, but part of me felt relieved knowing he was going to stir and inspire the prayers of the sisters and brothers.

For many years, the sisters and brothers used the hermitage and prayed with Christ the Merciful and Our Lady of Korsum. Over time, however, they began to leave for other countries, and gradually the hermitage fell into disuse. Thirty years after hosting its first visitor, it was closed and locked, and I had totally forgotten about the icons abandoned within.

Last year, a dear friend of the monastery who often helps us, mentioned completely out of the blue that he was looking for an icon called Christ the Merciful. He wished to have a version of this icon in his small Brooklyn apartment as a reminder of God's mercy and a window to prayer. The young man had never heard of my particular attachment to the Christ the Merciful icon. I had never told anyone. The mere mentioning of the words "Christ the Merciful" stirred joy within me and brought tears to my eyes; it brought back many vivid, personal memories of praying with the icon. Enthusiastically, I encouraged the young man to see about having our iconographer friend, Olga, paint this icon for him. She had painted another for him already, and he was pleased with her work. Besides, Olga is a dear friend and neighbor, a very special person to all of us, and her prices are very reasonable. She paints icons and teaches iconography simply out of love and devotion to the Lord.[7]

Then, while the young man was visiting and helping here one weekend, something totally out of the ordinary occurred. The thought came to me that he could take our reproduction home while his was being painted. There was one problem: I had forgotten where the icon was kept. Mentally, I went through every room in the monastery and the guesthouse, and knew Christ the Merciful was not in any of them. I also knew the icon had not left the premises; I had never given him away to anyone. With these thoughts in mind, I fell into a deep sleep that night. In the middle of the night, while I was totally asleep, I heard a distinct voice saying (or implying—whenever this phenomenon occurs, I try to remember the exact words, but it becomes impossible even though the message remains clear) the following: "The icon is in the hermitage. I want to be rescued and go home with the young man." Suddenly I woke up, stupefied. The inner voice and message was clear and to the point. There was no doubt and hesitation on my part. I knew what had to be done. I waited eagerly for daylight to arrive so I could act upon the matter.

Early that Sunday morning, when our guest and I met for breakfast just before the morning Office, I recounted the story to him. I urged that we go in great haste to the hermitage, before having breakfast or praying the Office. I felt a compelling urgency, but first I had to find the key for the hermitage door, for it had not been used in several years.

The hermitage is located a bit of a distance from the monastery, beyond the barn where our sheep seek shelter. We walked quickly down the hill. I was eager to reach the hermitage and retrieve the treasured icon. When we finally arrived and unlocked the door, we found everything immaculately clean. The last Little Brothers had left everything in perfect order, yet it had been three years or so since the hermitage was opened. I moved toward the oratory, where I expected to find the icon. To my great surprise, it was nowhere to be found. I was totally beside myself, looking everywhere, opening every drawer and closet door and checking every place the icon could possibly be. To my knowledge, the icon had never been removed from its prayerful spot in the hermitage, and I was pretty sure the brothers did not take it with them. Distraught, I said to the young man, "This can't be. The Lord has never disappointed me before. It always comes to pass when I hear an injunction like last night's."

As I was saying this, my right arm, seemingly on its own volition, began reaching to the top of the closet. I had no explanation for doing this, since I didn't see anything there from where I had been standing. I simply felt like someone was guiding my arm in that direction. I felt something. I brought it down, and we saw it was the icon of Christ the Merciful, the same icon I had not seen in so many years. I hastily dusted off the forgotten icon, and with almost trembling hands carried it back to the monastery. After a quick breakfast, I cleaned and waxed the icon, and the young man and I both went down to the chapel for the morning Office—indeed, in this case, an Office of thanksgiving! Slowly things began to make sense. I had wondered why the Lord had mentioned that he wished to be "rescued"; it hadn't made any sense to me. But after finding the icon, totally out of sight and forgotten on the top of a dusty closet, I understood: the Lord wanted to be rescued from the oblivion and neglect in which he was found. He wanted again to receive love and prayerful attention, and expected to find it in a small studio apartment in Brooklyn. Yes, it made perfect sense . . .

The story doesn't end there. One day after the icon departed for its temporary home, I was pondering what my next book would be about. I had been translating the Psalms and the Rule of Saint Benedict, but I saw those more as long-term projects. I kept praying for guidance and inspiration, and suddenly I heard and recognized the same inner voice, clearly and with the same certitude, saying, "The book shall be all about Christ and Christ the Merciful." The message was so clear and precise that I didn't have a doubt or hesitate for even an instant. My only concern, then and now, was "Lord, how can I do this? I am totally incapable of the task at hand, and utterly disqualified." Every time I sit down to write a chapter, this feeling of inadequacy descends on me, making me feel hopeless, and then something or someone arrives out of nowhere and the empty pages get filled. It is all a true mystery, something one experiences but can never explain. It is certainly true that the ways of God are mysterious and very much unlike our own. "O Merciful Christ, our Lord and Savior, your countless mercies I shall sing forever."

O Christ, my Savior, you have saved the prodigal son,
and you have shown compassion to the harlot woman.
Have mercy on me also, O most merciful Christ;
show your compassion and save me,
O Jesus, Benefactor of my soul,
even as you have shown compassion to Manasses,
for you are truly the Lover of mankind.

31.
Christ the Philanthropos
(Lover of Mankind)

I have loved you with an everlasting love; therefore I have continued my faithfulness to you.
            —Jeremiah 31:3

I pray that, according to the riches of his glory, he may grant that you may be strengthened in your inner being with power through his Spirit, and that Christ may dwell in your hearts through faith, as you are being rooted and grounded in love. I pray that you may have the power to comprehend, with all the saints, what is the breadth and length and height and depth, and to know the love of Christ that surpasses all knowledge, so that you may be filled with the fullness of God.
            —Ephesians 3:16–19

Love is from God; everyone who loves is born of God and knows God. Whoever does not love does not know God, for God is love. God's love was revealed among us in this way. God sent his only Son into the world so that we might live through him. In this is love, not that we loved God but that he loved us first and sent his Son to be the atoning sacrifice for our sins.

—1 John 4:7–10

Jesus knew that his hour had come to depart from this world and go the Father. Having loved his own who were in the world, he loved them to the end.

—John 13:1

In the liturgical language of the Oriental churches, Christ is often addressed as the "Lover of men" or the "Lover of mankind." For the Christians of the East, Christ is the embodiment of God's tenderness, of the Lord's ineffable love for his creatures. As the apostle John tells us, this love is the very essence of God's being. From the same apostle we learn that "love is from God; [and] everyone who loves is born of God and knows God. Whoever does not love does not know God, for God is love" (1 John 4:7–8). For the Christian, love is something more than a feeling. It is an awesome reality, the indescribable realization that love is God's essence, his very nature. God did not create love, as many believe; God himself is love. For God, love is a way of being himself.

God's love is all-inclusive. The Father manifested his love for his world by sending his only Son to sacrifice and give his life for the redemption of humankind. This is one reason why Christ is called the Lover of mankind. The apostle John helps us understand this deep truth by reminding us: "This is love, not that we loved God but that he loved us first and sent his Son to be the atoning sacrifice for our sins" (1 John 4:10).

In your abundant mercy,
O compassionate Lord and Lover of mankind,
you have called publicans, sinners, and unbelievers
to the banquet of eternal life.
Despise not our unworthiness,
but accept us into your loving company.

Christ's love is totally unconditional. The Word, the Father's Son, came into the world to invite every human to reconcile and enter into a loving relationship with the God who created each of us out of love. God has always expressed his utterly tender and loving care for each of his children. Now this love became totally visible in the person of his Son. Jesus, meek and gentle of heart, appears on earth willing to prove the mystery of God's unconditional love and forgiveness even to the hardest of hearts.

Fulfilling the words and pronouncements
of the God-bearing prophets, O Lover of mankind,
you did appear on earth and dwelt among men.
With your blessed coming you healed our wounds
and granted us great mercy.

Christ's love is sacrificial. Jesus laid down his life so that each of us may be forgiven and enter freely into a communion of love with his Father and our Father. Christ, the Lover of mankind, walked the extra mile and willingly accepted death, even death on a cross, so that mankind may be totally reconciled with God.

Christ, our Savior, Lover of mankind,
who brought all things into existence from nothing,
and with ineffable wisdom arranged for each of us to
*   accomplish the Father's will,*
fence and defend our lives with the mighty strength of
*   your love for mankind.*
Deliver us from corruption and the evil that threatens
*   us.*
For we are your servants, who place all our trust in you.

32.

Christ the Giver of Life

What has come into being in him was life, and the life was the light of all people.

—John 1:3–4

And this is the testimony: God gave us eternal life, and this life is in his Son. Whoever has the Son has life; whoever does not have the Son of God does not have life.

—1 John 5:11–12

You show me the path to life.
In your presence there is fullness and joy;
at your right hand are pleasures forevermore.

—Psalm 16:11

To be Christian, to believe in Christ means and has always meant this: to know in a trans-rational and yet absolutely certain way called faith, that Christ is the Life of all life, that He is Life itself, and therefore my life. "In him was life, and the life was the light of all men."
—Fr. Alexander Schmemann, *For the Life of the World*[8]

Ultimately, all search for life is the search for the person of Christ, the Author and Giver of life. Christ is a person, and that person is not only a vehicle to life, but life itself. As we reflect on God's words in the Gospels, we learn to penetrate ever more deeply into the mystery of Christ. As the mystery unfolds, it reveals to us that Christ and life are inseparably linked. In the Eastern Byzantine worship, Christ is addressed again and again as the Giver of life. This should not be a surprise to anyone, for what meaning is there to life itself outside Christ? Christ is our life. Any true life, life in abundance, is life in Christ—embracing all possible reality, both human and divine.

Jesus states in the Gospel, "I am the way, the truth, and the life." In a certain manner, Jesus is affirming that he is the way to the truth, and that once we reach the truth, we discover that real truth is life everlasting, the type of life that makes us totally free. The type of life Jesus offers is nothing like what we know here on earth, for what he offers and gives to his followers is eternal life—that is, fullness of life without death or fear of extinction.

Our Christian life is an affirmation that the Lover of mankind and Giver of life infuses into the very core of our being the seed of the eternal life he shares with the Father. Saint John, in his first letter, says, "And this is the testimony: God gave us eternal life, and this life is in his Son. Whoever has the Son has life; whoever does not have the Son of God does not have life" (1 John 5:11–12).

Each evening at Vespers, as we praise the Lord singing the hymn "Phos Hilaron," we address him as "Giver of life." It is a beautiful moment during our evening worship, for what we are actually doing is begging the Son to help us partake in that eternal life he shares with the Father. At the end of the hymn, as we praise and offer glory to the Father, the Son, and the Holy Spirit, we ask once more to be completely filled with the new life that Christ gained for his followers because of his death and resurrection.

O Christ, our true God,
you open to me the gates of repentance. O Giver of life,
my spirit rises early and gazes toward you,
bringing the temple of my body all defiled.
Since you are the all-compassionate one,
cleanse me by your compassionate mercy.

PART IV

CHRIST
in the Monastic Tradition

33.

The Gospel: A Guide for Monks

See, in His loving kindness, how the Lord shows us the way of life. Therefore, having our loins girt with faith and the performance of good works, let us walk His ways under the guidance of the Gospel, that we may be found worthy of seeing Him who hath called us to His kingdom.
—Rule of Saint Benedict, Prologue

Practice fasting; then meditate on the Gospel and the other Scriptures, and if an alien thought arises within you, never look at it but always look upwards, and the Lord will come at once to your help.
—Macarius the Great, Desert Father

We have found that through Christ's word: "I am the truth." This reality has become intrinsic to worship, and our fathers the Apostles used it in building the whole temple of Christian life. The truth of Christ is the Gospel; adhering to it is adhering to Christ.
—Matthew the Poor, a modern Desert Father

Since the life of the monk primarily consists in the imitation of Christ, the serious reading of, listening to, and study of the

Gospel is the most vital element of his monastic day. He seeks to shape his life by the teachings of Jesus, trying to follow with integrity and great fidelity even the smallest precepts of the Gospel, which leads to full knowledge of the revelation of God in Jesus Christ. It allows the monk to grow deeper and deeper into the *living experience* of him who reveals himself to the humble, the poor, the lowly, to the little ones.

For Saint Benedict, the monastery is "a school in the Lord's service," where the monk or nun learns to live according to the teachings of the Gospel. There is nothing more important for the monk, in the mind of Saint Benedict, than assimilating Christ through his Word in order to completely identify with him. He says the monk or nun must assiduously spend several hours a day in *lectio divina*, reading and meditating on the Sacred Scriptures—in particular, the Gospels. By fidelity to this practice, the monk brings his whole being, with all its powers and faculties, into a life-giving encounter with the revealed Word of God. Illumined by the Holy Spirit, he is nourished in the knowledge of God.

The reading, study, and prayerful pondering of the Word is a joint action of God and the monk: God speaks and the monk listens. And this interaction between the two is the work of the Holy Spirit.

> *O Christ, our Sun of righteousness,*
> *all darkness fades at your presence,*
> *a time for grace and pardon give.*
> *Send light to shine within our minds.*
> —"Iam, Christe, sol iustitiae," sixth-century hymn

34.
Following Christ: The Purpose of the Monastic Life

Jesus said to him, "If you wish to be perfect, go, sell your possessions, and give the money to the poor, and you will have treasure in heaven; then come, follow me."
—Matthew 19:21

The great ends of the monastic life can only be seen in the light of the mystery of Christ. Christ is the center of monastic living. He is the source and its end. He is the way of the monk as well as his goal.
—Thomas Merton, *The Monastic Journey*[9]

The words of Matthew 19:21 seized the heart of Saint Antony, the first monk, and transformed his life forever. The monk, touched by grace and seized by a love of Christ, slowly turns away from the ways of the world and wholeheartedly gives himself to following the Lord. Likewise today, Jesus invites us all to follow him into the desert of the monastic life.

The monastic life, consecrated exclusively to following Christ, is lived in a spirit of great simplicity, humility, and poverty, according to the Gospel. The monk wishes to follow the poor Christ, and to live in solidarity with those who still reveal him to us: the poor, the oppressed, the rejected, and the underprivileged people of the world. The spirit of the Beatitudes remains always the ideal for all monks. The monk has concrete ways of living out this identification with the poor. He goes about his manual work humbly. He joyfully accepts a diet that includes fasting and abstinence from meat, mindful that a great many people of the world are starving and exploited while society embraces affluence and waste. When he can, he gives individual assistance to those in need.

For Saint Benedict, obedience is key to imitating and following Christ. In Hebrews we learn of Jesus: "Although he was a Son, he learned obedience through what he suffered; and having been made perfect, he became the source of eternal salvation for all who obey him" (Heb. 5:8–9). For the love of Christ, the monk willingly accepts submission to the will of another human being—the abbot, according to the Rule of Saint Benedict—sacrificing his own will and desires in order to imitate more completely the example of his master and Savior. It is not the abbot alone, however. Saint Benedict goes a bit further, inviting the monks to obey one another, thus walking in the steps of Christ: "The brethren must render the service of obedience not only to the Abbot, but they must thus also obey one another, knowing that they shall go to God by this path of obedience."[10]

The monk hears the Lord's exhortation to lose his own life in order to gain it, and it is in the experience of this paradox that the monk mysteriously finds his ultimate fulfillment.

O Master, may I weep for nothing but only for sins,
may my only concern be for Your just sentence
and the means of my defense before my many offenses
  against You!
Yes, O compassionate Shepherd, so good and gentle!
You who wish to save all who believe in You,
have mercy, hear this my prayer.
Do not be angry, do not turn away from me Your face,
but teach me how to fulfill Your will.

—Saint Symeon the New Theologian, Hymn 47

35.
The Jesus Prayer

Lord Jesus Christ, Son of the living God, have mercy on me, a sinner.

—Jesus Prayer

The Jesus Prayer, by uniting us to Christ, helps us to share in the mutual indwelling or perichoresis of the three Persons of the Holy Trinity. The more the prayer becomes a part of ourselves, the more we enter into the movement of love which passes unceasingly between Father, Son, and Holy Spirit.

—Archimandrite Kallistos Ware

The connection between evangelical simplicity and the Jesus Prayer is an inner one. To truly pray the Jesus Prayer, we must first explore the depths of our hearts, where the action of grace can be felt. There, in the intimacy of our hearts, the Lord has established his own dwelling. Simplicity and interior silence make us aware of this divine presence within. It is from the awareness of this intimate presence within us that our prayer rises as a living whisper to God.

Simplicity and silence allow our minds and emotions to leave behind all distractions, daily turmoil, and present worries and concerns. Then, we can concentrate all our faculties on the divine guest who honors our innermost being with his presence. Through faith and an attitude of pristine simplicity, we come to understand the Lord's words: "The kingdom of God is among you" (Lk. 17:21). We need no longer look for him elsewhere, for he is indeed very close to us, right next to us, deep within us. And as we pray from the depths of our hearts, the Jesus Prayer becomes the key that unlocks the doors of the kingdom within.

Throughout the years, I have learned to approach the Jesus Prayer in two ways, with a view of it as a pilgrimage, and with an attitude of Gospel simplicity. Experiencing the Jesus Prayer in my earthly pilgrimage allows me to be rooted in the here and now, in the eternal present; this in turn finds its consummation in God's eternity. The Jesus Prayer is that precious link that connects and gives coherence and consistency to all life stages as they progress toward the eternal. An attitude of simplicity teaches me how to enter into the prayer. I say the prayer with my entire being, and yet do not become aware of what I am actually praying. Thus I absorb all the prayer's hidden riches. Gospel simplicity transforms all our senses, all our past memories and present feelings, including our innermost perceptions. It quietly reminds us of one thing: the presence of the Holy Spirit at work praying in us.

During those moments of intimate prayer, the Holy Spirit takes possession of our soul through his grace. His wonderful grace alerts us that we no longer belong to ourselves, but wholly to God alone. And as we struggle to pray, we are reminded of the apostle's words, that it is only through the power of the Holy Spirit that we are able to say or pray the sacred name of Jesus (see 1 Cor. 12:3). As Archimandrite Sophrony, a monastic father from our own times, explicitly tells us: "True prayer to the true God is contact with the Divine Spirit which prays in us. The Spirit gives us to know God. The Spirit draws us to contemplation of eternity."[11] Therefore, we often cry, "*Veni, Sancte Spiritus!*," begging the Spirit to help us pray.

The Jesus Prayer has its origins in the cry of the publican: "*Kyrie eleison*" ("Lord, have mercy"; see Lk. 18:13). The prayer, as it evolved throughout the centuries in the desert monastic tradition, gradually incorporated the holy name of Jesus itself and hence has become known as the Jesus Prayer. The prayer may be said in many ways, but basically consists of this very simple form: "*Lord Jesus Christ, Son of the living God, have mercy on me, a sinner.*" Could we ever find a prayer of greater depth and truth, and of such utter simplicity? It is one of the charms of the prayer: such brevity, yet so direct and containing a wealth within it.

The secret of the prayer lies in the continual recitation of the sweet name of Jesus. Just pronouncing the Lord's name fills me with a unique feeling of recollection and great peace, a peace that surpasses any earthly explanation and signifies to me his real presence. For this reason, throughout the centuries it has been a favorite method of praying for many monks and nuns, as well as for millions of lay Christians who have discovered its power. As an old monk used to quietly remind me: "In the prayer of the heart [as the Jesus

Prayer is also known], I have found my true rest, the place of my repose." He found in the continual recitation of the prayer not only rest, but also peace, consolation, strength, the secret to the practice of unceasing prayer; indeed, he found in the stillness produced by the prayer the very presence of the Lord himself.

One reason the Jesus Prayer is consoling is that it is a prayer of humble repentance. It allows us to encounter the Lord and cast our glance upon him in the present state in which we find ourselves: as sinners. There is no room for pretension or grandstanding in the prayer. Only by presenting ourselves before God as repentant sinners do we gain access to his infinite mercy. Repentance is not easy, and it is not always easy to chat about. Our world, today as in Jesus's time, has difficulty apprehending the mystery of repentance. Neither does it grasp its Gospel significance. We live in a society that pretends to be just and virtuous. We are so self-righteous that we would consider it an insult if anyone called us or considered us sinners. And yet the Jesus Prayer originates in a humble act of repentance, and it demands true repentance from us. As we enter into the prayer, we acknowledge our sinfulness with great simplicity, and repent for the actual sins of our past and present life. Furthermore, we pray that the Holy Spirit may grant us the grace to repent with our whole being.

While we are in this life, repentance is the secret door of the Jesus Prayer. We need not to go too far; all true prayer begins in the very place where we stand. And that very real place, our sinful state, is where God is ready to meet us, to welcome us, to forgive us. All we need then is to enter into ourselves with great simplicity and cry out with humble repentance: *"Lord Jesus Christ, Son of the living God, have mercy on me, a sinner."* The more often we do this, the sooner and the better we shall discover God's gracious and loving presence in us. The more the mystery of repentance grasps our inner self, the more we shall be able to behold Christ and cling to his saving garment. During our earthly pilgrimage, as we walk the humble way of repentance while never ceasing to pray the sacred name, the Lord Jesus becomes present to us. He becomes then our sole reality, our intimate friend, and the one straight path to the Father, for, he says, "No one comes to the Father except through me" (John 14:6).

The Jesus Prayer is a dependable, faithful companion to the monk at all times. It becomes a home to us everywhere, wherever we may be; it travels well. It is a rest, a solace, and at all times a point of convergence. The prayer, always short and to the point, presents in stark simplicity the reality of our inner life. Anyone who wishes to pray it can do so at any time, even when falling asleep. The prayer's repetition doesn't make it mechanical. If so, it would lose its intrinsic value.

There is a double movement in the prayer, and both parts are fundamental to it. First, we address ourselves directly to our Lord Jesus Christ, and we acknowledge him as God and Savior, the all merciful one. We breathe deeply and rest there, in his presence, counting on the power of his name to make up for our insufficiencies and sinfulness. This is the first movement of the prayer, to which we return over and over again. The second movement concerns us, the reality of who we are and the state in which we find ourselves while praying to God: poor sinners in dire need of God's abundant mercy. Jesus is the infinitely merciful one, and we must become a living replica of the repentant publican from the Gospel. The prayer, as it gets repeated over and over, becomes an interplay back and forth between these two movements, a cycle from which we never wish to leave. Gradually, the prayer takes complete hold of us. Then, it goes on day and night, no matter what activity or state we may find ourselves in. As we fall asleep with the prayer deeply grounded in our hearts, we know the invocation of the holy name will be the waking sound on our lips and in our hearts as we once again start our daily routine: *"Lord Jesus Christ, Son of the living God, have mercy on me, a sinner."*

Pray night and day.
Pray when you are happy
and pray when you are sad.
Pray with fear and trembling,
and with a watchful and vigilant mind,
that your prayer might be acceptable to the Lord,
for as the Scriptures say:
"The eyes of the Lord are on the righteous,
and his ears are open to their appeal."
　　　　　—Theodoros the Great Ascetic

36.
A Christ-Centered Life:
Saint Benedict

With the Gospel for our guide, may we deserve to see him who has called us to his kingdom.
—Prologue of the Rule of Saint Benedict

From the start, every page of Saint Benedict's Rule is imbued with the presence of the authentic Christ from the Gospels. From the opening prologue, Saint Benedict leads the disciple directly to the source and reason for the Rule. He gently summons the disciple to incline the ear of his heart, to listen attentively, to undertake the noble weapon of obedience, in order to do battle for the true King, Christ the Lord. He presents the disciple with the mystery of the person of Christ who alone is the source of our faith and who alone can provide true nourishment for our inner life.

For Saint Benedict, Christ is the starting point, the in-between, and the end point. The unfolding of the Rule has no other purpose but to lead the disciple to encounter this Christ of the Gospels, the living Christ, the Christ who offers himself to us in the simplicity and humility of his humanity. The Gospels contain the mystery of the Word. By faithfully listening with the heart's ears to every utterance and learning to live by them, the disciple can begin to discover and enter into the mystery of him who is the Way, the Truth, and the Life. As Raymond Brown used to remind us in his lectures at Union Theological Seminary (which I had the privilege to attend from time to time), Christ is the way because he teaches the truth, and this leads to the true life.

After the prologue, as we go on reading and meditating on each sentence from the Rule, we arrive at the fourth chapter, and there we find a sentence that seems to summarize the entire work. Straightforwardly and with moving simplicity, Saint Benedict emphatically counsels the disciple to "prefer nothing to the love of Christ."[12] For Saint Benedict, our entire human-Christian existence, the entire monastic ethos, exists only to point to Christ, the Alpha and the Omega. All things in time and in daily life are ordered to achieve this end: the perseverance of the disciple in the intense activity of loving his master, Christ the Lord. For Saint Benedict, the love of Christ is the only goal and purpose of the monastic life. The disciple learns that through loving Christ above all else, all things are possible in his otherwise humble and simple monastic life. He also learns the contrary: that without Christ his monastic life makes no sense.

The monastic life traces its origins to the Gospels. In the Scriptures, we learn that Christ invites disciples to leave all possessions aside in order to follow him—not only material objects, but also marriage and a normal family life, the freedom to move and do as he or she pleases, and his or her own will. To follow Christ means to forsake all for the imitation of Christ's own life, embracing the simplicity of the Gospels in its totality. This Gospel simplicity is a form of dedicated love, a creative expression and imitation of him who emptied himself to assume our humanity out of love for each of us. Through embracing this Gospel simplicity, Saint Benedict teaches the disciple to penetrate the very life of God himself, which is divine love. For God is love, and Jesus Christ, his Son, is the ultimate manifestation of this love.

As a wise master of the spiritual life, Saint Benedict designed the monastic daily journey from Vigils to Compline to be such that its every moment and circumstance will give the monk or nun the occasion to come close to Christ, to touch him and to be touched by him. The liturgy and its Offices, the *lectio divina*, the times of silent prayer, the daily manual or intellectual work, the meetings among the brethren and the guests, the interchanges with the abbot who takes the place of Christ in the monastery: all are real occasions for the monastic to personally encounter Christ.

Through every particle of the Rule, Saint Benedict wishes to transmit to the disciple his attachment to the person of Christ and to help make this attachment the disciple's own. He often cites Saint Paul, and this should not come as a surprise. The Christocentric character of the letters of Saint Paul held an appeal for Saint Benedict second only to the words of the Lord in the Gospels. Saint Benedict certainly made Paul's words his own: "For me, to live is Christ." For the humble Benedict, the only thing that truly mattered was that at all times and in all occasions he would find himself to be "in Christ."

The love and knowledge of Jesus Christ experienced in the depths of our hearts inexorably leads us to the experience and knowledge of the Father's love for all and each of us. There lies the great mystery. Christ introduces us to that intimate communion of love that he shares with the Father and the Holy Spirit. To be "in Christ," to abide in him permanently, therefore means to share in this intimate relationship with the three divine Persons. Saint Benedict impregnates the disciple with the certainty that in Christ all things are brought together, that through him alone the ultimate realities of God's saving actions are rendered present to the whole world. As Saint Paul assures us, "if anyone is in Christ, there is a new creation" (2 Cor. 5:17). For the disciple, as for Saint Benedict, this means to be absorbed in Christ, to think and to act like him. Furthermore, it means to live in a perpetual, loving, intimate relationship with him. The summit of all mystical life, according to Saint Symeon the New Theologian, is precisely this personal encounter with Christ, who in turn shows us the Father and continues to speak in our hearts through the Holy Spirit.

The many long years of living under the Rule—of trying to digest Saint Benedict's thoughts and absorb his teachings—have shown me that there is a strong pedagogical bent to the Rule, a unity based on the unique intuition of Saint Benedict himself. From the beginning of the Rule to the very last chapter, Saint Benedict gradually and with utter simplicity and insight introduces the disciple to true Gospel living. Chapter after chapter puts forth one of the many distinct aspects of a true evangelical life.

For Saint Benedict, the Gospel and the person of Christ are inseparable. The Gospel is the Book of Life: the Christ of Bethlehem and the Christ of the Cross, the Christ of the Eucharist and the Christ of the Resurrection, are all present in the Gospel. We discover Christ in his childhood years; Christ in his hidden life in Nazareth with Mary and Joseph; Christ teaching in the Temple in Jerusalem; Christ gathering his disciples; Christ preaching throughout Judea and Jerusalem; Christ praying long nights in the desert solitude; Christ healing the sick and nourishing the multitude; Christ the friend of Mary, Martha, and Lazarus; Christ proclaiming the Beatitudes; Christ undergoing his passion and resurrection on the third day; Christ ascending to his Father while promising to send us the Comforter.

When the Gospel is proclaimed during our daily offices and worship, we are captured, so to speak, by Christ's mysterious presence. The events of the past and the present somehow converge in the actual presence of Christ in the *today* of God. When Saint Benedict counsels the disciple to "walk in the ways of the Gospel," he is inviting him to enter into this profound mystery of Christ ever-present in his Word. The Christian journey, the monastic journey, consists precisely in this daily discovery of Christ the Logos, the Word, as present in the Gospels. There, we discover him and we touch the hem of his garments; we listen to his voice while quietly absorbing his teachings; we learn to eat of his body and drink of his blood while we ourselves are assimilated by him in the Eucharist. What is more, in this process of assimilation we are transformed into him.

When Saint Benedict decided to "establish a school for the Lord's service," he had in mind a particular way of learning and guiding the disciple. The disciple's entire life was directed exclusively to acquiring the knowledge of Jesus Christ and constantly growing in it. There is no confusion in the Rule: this intimate friendship with Christ is what sustains every moment of the disciple's daily life. He gradually learns, as Benedict points out, "to share through patience in the sufferings of Christ" so that one day he may deserve to share in the joys of his kingdom. The disciple learns to let go of his own plans and expectations and seek only the path of Christ's commandments and the inexpressible delight of his love. As Thomas Merton beautifully expresses, "The monastic life is life in the Spirit of Christ, a life in which the Christian gives himself entirely to the love of God which transforms him in the light of Christ."[13] All else is rubbish and of no consequence to the disciple.

There is a timeless appeal in Saint Benedict's particular approach to pursuing a Christ-centered life. Some may think that such a life can only apply to those who embrace the monastic path. I think Saint Benedict would be the first to disagree with that perception. Saint Benedict, who once had a vision of a luminous globe like the sun containing everything and everyone in it, in God, never envisioned a special caste of people as followers of Christ, and neither did the Desert Fathers and Mothers. They were simple lay Christians who wanted to follow the radical path of the Gospel without any encumbrances. This desire to follow Christ closely led them to the solitude of the wilderness, or, in the case of Saint Benedict, to the solitude of Subiaco. They never intended to found a so-called religious or monastic order. When lay disciples gathered around him and asked him to be their leader, Saint Benedict made recourse to a Rule as a unifying principle. Because the Rule was so simple, sober, and balanced in all aspects, it went on to become what it is today: a way of intensely living one's Christian life, a Gospel way of following Christ.

Throughout the centuries, new ways of following Christ—new Christian movements and even new religious orders—have emerged. Interestingly, they each seem to emphasize one aspect of the Gospel message, or of Christian spirituality. This would have been incomprehensible to Saint Benedict and the early desert monks and nuns. It is incomprehensible today to Eastern Christians and those who follow the monastic life in the tradition of the early Eastern churches. For them all, there is only one spirituality and one way of living: that of the entire Gospels. Nowhere in the early Christian tradition was there a need to emphasize one aspect of a Christ-centered life over another. This tendency developed in the Christian West and became stronger after the separation of the Eastern and Western churches in 1054. Today we live with this ambivalence, with endless interpretations, variations, and ramifications of the Gospel message—when in fact it is all one.

Therein lies the wisdom of Saint Benedict, today as it was in his times: the unity of Christ as revealed in the Gospels, above all realized in the intimate relationship of the disciple with his master, Christ the Lord. As Saint Benedict understood, there is nothing sweeter to the disciple than to undertake the Lord's yoke and the pure constraints of the Gospel. By accepting to live daily in all purity, humility, charity, and Gospel simplicity, the disciple can't help but have a small impact upon his surrounding world. His is the privilege of exuding "the sweet odor of Christ" to all those who approach him or come close to him.

O Christ, our God,
we praise you for the example of Saint Benedict's holy
   life.
His one concern was to follow you to the end,
and to please God alone.
May we follow the wisdom path of his teachings
by preferring Christ above all things,
and by choosing the Gospel as our sole guide.

37.

Christ, the Serenity of Monks

Do not fret because of the wicked;
do not be envious of wrongdoers,
for they will soon fade like grass
and wither like the green herb.
Trust in the LORD, *and do good;*
so you will live in the land, and enjoy security.
Take delight in the LORD,
and he will give you the desires of your heart.
Be still before the LORD,
and wait patiently for him.
—Psalm 37:1–4, 7a

*Detach yourself from the love of the multitude, lest your
enemy question your spirit and trouble your inner serenity.*
—Abba Douglas

*When we have celebrated our first Sabbath in the seren-
ity of our hearts, we can go on to consider how this heart
of ours must be enlarged so as to become a great shelter,
a haven in which to welcome all who have need of our
sympathy when they are sorrowful, or who would have
us rejoice with them when they are glad.*
—Saint Aelred of Rievaulx, *The Mirror of Charity*

The humble Saint Seraphim of Sarov once said, "Keep your heart serene, and thousands will find salvation around you." He was addressing himself to monks and non-monks alike—in other words, to all Christians. Saint Seraphim knew intuitively how much the world and the church of his times were in dire need of peaceful serenity. He expected somehow that this state of inner serenity could emerge from monasteries, from the hearts of monks, possessed in their innermost by the intimate presence of Christ.

The vocation of a monk is a vocation to the center of all reality, where Christ dwells. A monk by his humble calling is led by the Holy Spirit to enter, live, and remain in the center, and that center is Christ. With Christ, by God's grace, the monk finds the inner peace, the serenity, to stick with and persevere on that path that leads to eternal life—that is, a totally God-centered life.

If the monk is serious about pursuing serenity, one of the first things he must do is bring all useless activities to a halt. A radical life change is a must; otherwise, nothing of substance is achieved. Throughout the toils of the monastic day, its cycles of prayer and work, the monk must never lose sight of his one and only goal: constant communion with Christ. It is by re-centering his life totally in Christ—"hidden with Christ in God," in the words of Saint Paul (Col. 3:3)—that the monk avoids anxiety and turbulence, thus achieving a peaceful life full of love and joy, serenity and tranquility, which are the gifts of a God-centered life.

Ultimately, the monk's serenity is of great hope to others and to the world at large. Often, our world finds itself in a state of failure and confusion, in a deplorable state of chaos. The serenity of the monk, then, which springs forth from the heart of Christ, offers to others the possibility of looking at life through a different lens—through God's light, which illumines our darkness and which redeems our poor, limited human perspective.

O Lord our God, my Savior Jesus Christ,
Place a seal on my senses by your gift of stillness,
Then sit in judgment over my thoughts,
Which make a noisy clamor in my heart.
— Thalassios the Libyan

38.

The Monk's Attachment to Christ

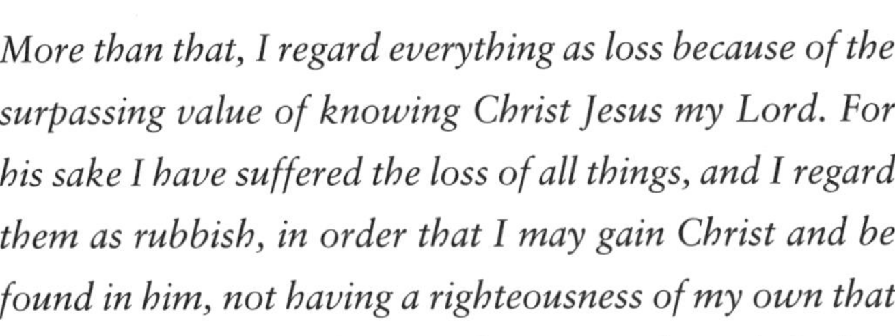

More than that, I regard everything as loss because of the surpassing value of knowing Christ Jesus my Lord. For his sake I have suffered the loss of all things, and I regard them as rubbish, in order that I may gain Christ and be found in him, not having a righteousness of my own that comes from the law, but one that comes through faith in Christ, the righteousness from God based on faith.
—Philippians 3:8–9

Withdraw from the world means two things:
the withering away of our obsessions
and the revelation of the life that is hidden in Christ.
—Theodore the Ascetic

Monastic life is all about getting to know Christ, getting ever closer to the Lord, and thus deepening our life in him. Saint Benedict, in his wisdom, tells us that Christ alone is the source of our faith and the true nourishment of our souls, and he presses the disciple to prefer nothing to Christ and his mystery. From day one in the monastery, the disciple is invited to realize that, without Christ, his monastic life offers no meaning and makes no sense. Daily, little by little, the young monastic is urged to discover this Christ—his teachings and what his life was like while on earth. He is then urged to try, slowly, to begin imitating him. This is what was called by the ancient monastics the *sequela Christi* or the *imitatio Christi*. At this point in the monk's early journey, he discovers the treasure he possesses in the Gospels, and begins to drink from that living fountain. In the very prologue of the Rule, Saint Benedict makes this teaching clear to the disciple: "With the Gospel as our guide, may we deserve to see him who has called us into his kingdom."[14] Daily, monks pray to the Theotokos, God's Mother, to increase in them a tender and loving attachment to the person of her Son, Christ our Lord and Savior. *Mihi vivere Christus est.*

Come, You who have become my desire
and have me desire You, the Inaccessible One.
Come, my breath, my life.
Come, consolation of my poor soul.
Come, my joy, my glory, my endless delight.
For I must give you all my thanks
for making yourself one with my spirit.
        —Saint Symeon the New Theologian

39.

Christ, Our Mystical Supper
(A Monastic Perspective)

*Be zealous, then, in the observance of one Eucharist.
For there is one flesh, Our Lord, Jesus Christ, and one
Chalice that brings union in his Blood.*
> —Saint Ignatius of Antioch

*At sunset, on the day of the Holy Last Supper of the
Lord, bring me the life-giving Body and Blood of Christ
in a holy vessel worthy of such mysteries, and wait for
me on the bank of the Jordan, on the inhabited side,
so that I can receive and make my communion with
the life-giving gifts. From the time on when I made my
communion in the church of the Holy Precursor, before
crossing the Jordan and entering into the desert, up
to this day I have not received the Holy Sacraments.
And now I hunger for it with a love which cannot be
restrained. This is why I beg and implore of you to fulfill
my request.*
> —*Life of Saint Mary of Egypt*, her last request
> to the monk Zossima

Holy Thursday commemorates the institution of the Eucharist. Each year, as I approach the evening celebration that commemorates the Lord's Supper, I recall this is a profound mystery, *mysterium tremendum*, a mystery not to trivialize or take lightly, a mystery that must never become routine or taken for granted. After having been purified by the holy fast and Lenten observances, one can now reach the table of the Lord with a sincere heart and humble mind. All things converge into the Lord's sacred Passover meal, the mystical supper, the heavenly banquet to which all those looking for salvation are invited. Behold, this is truly the time of our salvation, in which the Lord's divine gifts, poured lavishly into our lives, are at our disposal. In that blessed night of Holy Thursday, the night anticipating his hour, the Lord left us the gift of himself as testament of his boundless love. He loved us until the very end, as the Gospels tell us, and at the end he had no more to give but himself.

The early church, the Desert Fathers and Mothers—indeed, Saint Benedict himself—did not have the option of daily Eucharist as it has now become the practice in most places in the Western Church. On Sundays they all received the body and blood of the Lord. It took them all week to prepare themselves for its reception, and then another in thanksgiving for having partaken of the divine gifts and its assimilation into their lives. These early disciples of the Lord approached the sacred mysteries with such seriousness and utter reverence that for them it could never have become a daily routine. For them, the Lord's Eucharistic mysteries could never be measured in terms of time. They hungered for him all week long, and once they received him in the mystery of Communion, they felt totally possessed by him, incorporated into his very body. Now, they were part of him and he was part of them. Therefore, nothing in time could separate them from him. This mystical but very real exchange is the essence of the Eucharist. It is ineffable, transcendent, and inexplicable. In the quotation above, Saint Mary of Egypt, days before dying, expresses vividly this real hunger for the divine mysteries. Weekly Eucharist is still the practice of the Eastern church and Eastern monasteries, often preceded by this beautiful prayer from Saint Basil:

Of your mystic supper, O Son of God, receive me today
as a communicant;
for I will not speak of the mystery to your enemies;
nor will give You a kiss like Judas.
But like a thief I confess You: Remember me, O Lord,
in your kingdom.
Remember me, O Master, in your kingdom.
Remember me, O Holy One, in your kingdom.

PART V

CHRIST
in the Human Family

40.

Jesus, Child of Mary
the God-Bearer

When his parents saw him they were astonished; and his mother said to him, "Child, why have you treated us like this? Look, your father and I have been searching for you in great anxiety."

He said to them, "Why were you searching for me? Did you not know that I must be in my Father's house?" But they did not understand what he said to them. Then he went down with them and came to Nazareth, and was obedient to them. His mother treasured all these things in her heart.

—Luke 2:48–51

Since you are a living temple of God, O Theotokos, no malicious hand shall ever touch you. Let the lips and hearts of believers ceaselessly praise you, crying unto you joyfully with the song of the angels: Truly, O Most Pure Virgin, you are highly exalted above all creatures.

—Byzantine Matins for Our Lady's
Presentation in the Temple

We as Christians and disciples of Jesus can learn from the simplicity we encounter in Mary, his Mother. She is a living example of Gospel simplicity. I would go so far as asserting that she is simplicity personified. The image of Mary in the Gospels stands against all that is false, haughty, selfish, and arrogant. Her presence alone dissipates the forces of darkness and evil. The moment she receives the good news from the archangel Gabriel about the mission God intends for her, she accepts her role with infinite humility and simplicity. She doesn't attribute anything to herself. She is the humble and obedient servant of the Lord. Filled with the beauty and strength of her own simplicity, she accepts lovingly the Lord's design for her: "Here am I, the servant of the Lord; let it be with me according to your word" (Lk. 1:38). She demands nothing from Gabriel, God's messenger; on the contrary, she accepts everything, and in return she receives everything. The Word becomes flesh in her, and the Son of God becomes also the son of Mary. She who was poor and powerless—the true *anawim*—now possesses all: God himself. From now on, all generations shall call her blessed.

We call her our Lady, the Theotokos, Queen of Heaven, and yet Mary continues to refer to herself simply as "the servant of the Lord." What profound lessons about true simplicity we can all learn from her! She shows us the way to complete surrender and submission to God's will. Like Mary, we too are called daily to utter our "yes" to God not once, but many times. And like Mary, our model of Gospel living, we must do so in total simplicity, with complete humility, and trusting in God's plan for us.

Christians, and also many non-Christians, are aware of the unique role that Mary plays in the Catholic and Orthodox traditions. Long before the apostles brought the Good News to the four corners of the world, veneration of she who gave birth to God, Mary Most Holy, was integral to the early Jerusalem church. Some of the early disciples knew Mary personally and kept her loving memory alive among the rapidly increasing number of Jesus's followers. The Gospels describe the unique place assigned to the Mother of God in the unfolding mystery of our salvation. She is present from the very beginning, Gabriel's announcement of the glad tidings of the Savior's incarnation, to the end, at the foot of the cross.

The New Testament gives us few facts about Mary. The Evangelists Matthew and Luke relate events concerning the Incarnation and the birth of the Savior in Bethlehem, including some brief information about his early years in Nazareth. In the Gospel of John, we find brief mentions of Mary: at Cana, and later standing at the foot of the cross. In Acts we find her quiet presence in the midst of the apostles at that first Pentecost. In the remaining New Testament books, her presence is obscured, if it exists at all. It is not as if the early church wanted to keep quiet about Mary or her role during those developmental years. First of all, the Evangelist John, the apostle to whom Jesus entrusted the care of his Mother, tells us that there are many things that Jesus did about which little or nothing is written. From this we can logically conclude that there was much more to Mary, the chosen Mother of the Savior, but that for whatever reason the Evangelists kept a respectful silence about her.

In many ways, by telling us too little about Jesus's Mother, they say a lot. As the old Spanish proverb suggests, "To him of good understanding, few words suffice." Furthermore, the life of the Mother was spent in the shadow of the mystery of her divine Son. How could anyone, except the angels perhaps, say anything worthy of the sublime intimacy between these two? There is a hint here and there from the way Jesus addresses her respectfully, mannerly: "Woman"—or the way Mary addresses Jesus after he is found in the Temple or during the Cana wedding. So much of what transpired between Jesus and Mary, between Mother and Son, remains as it should: under the veil of lofty mystery. Shouldn't we also try to capture something of that sublime, unique, and tender love experience that existed between Mother and Son?

I think our very personal love for her son, Jesus, is the source and reason for the veneration and love we have for our Lady. As we discover and fall in love with Christ, who gave his life to save us, we also come to the marvelous discovery of she who gave him that very life, thus making possible our salvation. Only God, in his boundless love for humankind, could have formulated or imagined such a divine enterprise. *O Magnum Mysterium!*

The veneration of Mary permeates the history of Christianity. Some emphasize her perpetual virginity, others her immaculate conception, still others her dormition—passing from earthly life—and glorious assumption to heaven. Some emphasize the fact that she is the Panagia, the "all-holy one." The most significant role to me, the one that summarizes Mary's privileges and her supreme role in the plan of salvation, is that of Theotokos or "God-bearer." The early church, assembled in solemn council at Ephesus in 431, declared her so. From then on, all Christians, both Eastern and Western, are called to rightly proclaim her the Mother of God—the one who is intimately connected to the mystery of Jesus Christ, her Son, the mystery that was in God's mind before time began. In many ways, as the church develops and continues to grow, it mirrors itself more and more in the image of Mary, the Theotokos.

Our Lady becomes, in a sense, the perfect "icon" of what the church is called to be: a living worship of love and adoration to the triune God. The Holy Spirit was fully at work in Mary during and after the Incarnation. The Church today is also called to live infused with the Holy Spirit. Mary is the one in whom the Word came to dwell and take flesh, and thus through her become impregnated in our own humanity. And so the church is to be the very body of Christ by living and witnessing to the truths of the Gospel. Mary, the Theotokos, shares with God the unique privilege of making Christ, the Word Incarnate, fully present to our world for the sake of our salvation.

The mystery of the Theotokos is embedded within the mystery of her Son; therefore, she remains very dear to us, his followers. The Christian faithful, in particular monks and nuns immersed in their contemplative silence, ponder this mystery daily with admiration, while all along realizing it is totally beyond their comprehension. Our monasteries and hermitages are usually ornamented with icons of the Mother of God, reminding us of her quiet presence in our midst. In most icons of her, Mary is portrayed carrying the child Jesus in her arms. While the eyes of Jesus rest lovingly upon his Mother, her gaze is directed tenderly toward us and toward all those who approach him. With her charming, incomparable simplicity, Mary shows her Son to each of us, silently whispering in our ears, "Behold your God, who has become a child for you."

In the Gospels, the Theotokos is always depicted in physical closeness to Jesus, pointing directly to him. In her Magnificat, Mary's song of praise, she refers to herself as "God's humble handmaid," showing us the utter depths of a total self-effacing attitude before the immeasurableness of Jesus Christ. She makes no claims to herself. She is only the simple, humble creature who bore the Son of God in time. She acknowledges that it is God alone who has done great things in her. It is therefore right, Mary would urge, that our obedience and the undivided attention of our hearts belong to God alone.

We rejoice as we discover that Mary is both God's Mother and our own. She adopted us at the foot of the cross when Jesus said to her, referring to the disciple John, "Woman, here is your son" (John 19:26). In the person of John, each of us also becomes a child of Mary. Filled as she is with God's own light, Mary knows God's loving designs for each of us and she whispers them gently, daily, in our ears. She knows God's plans for us, and our weaknesses, how slow we often are in following God's ways. As a tender and always helpful Mother, she is there, present to us, very close by, always ready to come to our rescue, more concerned about our eternal salvation than are we ourselves. And her motherly concern is not limited to us: it extends to the whole world, to the entire universe. Like her son, she is particularly concerned for the poor, for the abandoned, for the unwanted, for the suffering, and for those who have no one to help them. Mary, the Theotokos, is always there for them.

From the very moment of our baptism, as we become fully incorporated into the body of Christ, Mary's presence becomes very real. She is our Mother, our friend, our solace, our helper, our refuge in time of danger, and our consolation in time of distress. We look to Mary during periods of darkness to be our luminous guide and our hope in the midst of despair. As we journey toward God's kingdom, Mary's warm presence dispels our feelings of loneliness. She, the Theotokos, gives the needed strength and courage to complete the journey. We walk as Christians but never alone, for the Mother of God is always by our side. If we learn to remain quiet, live by Gospel simplicity, and don't fuss too much about ourselves, we should be able to sense her continually consoling presence as we take each step on the road to God's kingdom.

> *Holy Mother of God,*
> *by the example of your pure simplicity*
> *and your utter humility*
> *you attracted the eyes of the Lord*
> *and touched the depths of his heart.*
> *Inspire us to follow in your footsteps,*
> *that we may also please him*
> *all the days of our earthly life.*

41.

Jesus, Son of Joseph the Righteous

Joseph, Son of David, do not be afraid to take Mary as your wife, for the child conceived in her is from the Holy Spirit. She will bear a son, and you are to name him Jesus, for he will save his people from their sins.
—Matthew 1:20–21

Tell us, Joseph, how is it that you bring to Bethlehem,
  great with child,
the Maiden whom you have received from the sanctuary?
"I have searched the prophets," said he, "and have been
  warned by an angel;
and I am persuaded that Mary shall give birth to God,
  in ways surpassing all understanding.
Magi from the East shall come to worship Him with
  precious gifts."
O Lord, who for our sake have taken flesh: Glory to You.
—Byzantine Offices for Christmas Eve

During our annual Advent pilgrimage in the liturgies of both the East and the West, we encounter figures who help us comprehend something of the mystery of the Incarnation:

our Lady, the Theotokos; Gabriel, the bearer of the good news; ancient prophets and patriarchs; John the Precursor and his parents; and last but not least, Saint Joseph, the righteous man.

After our Lady, it is Joseph, the humble carpenter from Nazareth, who plays the greatest role in the birth and rearing of the child Jesus. Joseph is commanded by the angel to protect and safeguard the life of the tiny child and his Mother. His role during the birth of Christ is ignored by many because of his unostentatious manner: not a single utterance of his is recorded in the Gospel account of the Nativity. Joseph was concerned only with giving his undivided attention to Jesus and Mary. He is, above all, a humble servant of the Lord. In our daily Christian lives, he is a sure model of what we are called to be. Like Mary, in giving his complete obedience to the Lord, he paradoxically receives the Son of God's complete obedience to him.

Joseph comes across in the Gospels as quiet, hidden, almost inconsequential. An angel encourages him to put aside all his fears regarding Mary's mysterious pregnancy and accept what the Holy Spirit has worked in her. His vocation is now elevated as he shares and partakes in the unfolding mystery. Joseph clearly understands that Mary's pregnancy is not a source of shame but an act of God. She and the child are now entrusted to his loving care. With the help of the angel, Joseph learns to overcome his fears, his perplexity, his earthly concerns, discovering a new way of relating to God in complete faith. Furthermore, the angel gives Joseph the unique assignment of being the one to name the Son of God "Jesus."

In Mary and Joseph, the Lord found all his pleasure. He trusted them completely. The example of faith, humility, and obedience that God knew in them should open our own inner eyes and inspire our daily pursuit to discern God's will in our own lives. Like Mary and Joseph, we are called to interiorly nurture Christ—his life in us—daily, humbly, faithfully. May the Theotokos and her holy bridegroom Joseph watch over us, that somehow our spiritual lives may reflect theirs, thus pleasing God.

> *Because you loved purity of heart, you became a close*
> *friend of God.*
> *He has chosen you to be the foster-father of His only*
> *Son.*
> *The ever-virgin Mary was entrusted to you as a pure*
> *bride,*
> *therefore you received the choicest gifts of the Holy*
> *Spirit.*
> *O holy Joseph, intercede for the salvation of our souls.*
>
> *We venerate your blessed memory, O Joseph,*
> *the Gospels themselves praise your name.*
> *You are the humble man who gained eternal fame,*
> *by caring for Jesus and Mary.*
> *Teach us the way to heaven, O Joseph, and be our guide.*
> —Byzantine Sticheras for Saint Joseph's Feast

42.
Christ, Our Hope

In Christ we have also obtained an inheritance, having been destined according to the purpose of him who accomplishes all things according to his counsel and will, so that we, who were the first to set our hope in Christ, might live for the praise of his glory.
—Ephesians 1:11–12

One of the themes that prevails during my Advent meditations is hope. During Advent we are invited to relive the hope of ancient Israel as it waited and longed for the Messiah, for him who would bring deliverance to God's chosen people. Sacred Scripture, especially the writing of the prophets, inspires us to enter into that expectant hope that nurtured the faith of the people of Israel. Hope is a theological virtue, a gift from the Holy Spirit, one that fills our souls with joyful anticipation for the Desired One of our hearts. In the midst of the gloom, greed, and deadly materialism of our present times, we await in hope, for we know the Lord is truly coming and he shall free us from personal despair and slavery, as he did once with the Israelites.

During our Advent days—and, by extension, all year round—we delight in rediscovering the fact that the source of our hope is not an abstract attitude, belief, or virtue; it is a person: Christ, the Lord. And we know that he is all love, all goodness, all mercy, the pure reflection of God's glory. Furthermore, through the grace and action of the Holy Spirit, Christ lives and acts in us, and it is hope that makes us more alert, more vigilant, somehow fully awake and ever grateful for his real presence in our lives. Jesus, the God-man, is the sure anchor of our hope of glory, and he promised to be always with us until the end of time: *Christus, spes nostra*. In the words of one of the Advent seasonal antiphons: "Eagerly we await the fulfillment of our hope, the glorious coming of our Savior."

God is Light,
the Most High, the Unapproachable,
God cannot be conceived in the mind
or spoken by the lips.
God is the Life-Giver for every rational creature.
God is to the world of spiritual intellect
what the sun is to the sensory world,
and will manifest divinity in our minds
to the degree that we are purified.
　　　　　　　—Saint Gregory Nazianzus

43.

Christ, Lover of the Poor

Have among yourselves the same attitude that is also yours in Christ Jesus, Who, though he was in the form of God, did not regard equality with God something to be grasped. Rather, he emptied himself, taking the form of a slave, coming in human likeness.

—Philippians 2:5–7 (NABRE)

Love is the kingdom of which our Lord spoke symbolically when He promised his disciples that they would eat in His kingdom: "You shall eat and drink at the table in My kingdom." What would they eat, if not love? . . . When we have reached love, we have reached God and our way is ended: we have passed over to the island that lies beyond the world, where the Father is with the Son and the Holy Spirit: to Whom be glory and dominion forever.

—Saint Isaac the Syrian, *Mystic Treatises*

A frequent theme in Christ's public ministry was embracing real poverty, a self-emptying state. "Blessed are the poor of spirit," he often said to his disciples. In another context he reminded them, "The poor you will always have with you," as if to say, "In the poor you will always be able to find me." Christ's admonition challenged the disciples then, as it does today's Christians, who often overlook this hard-to-take teaching. It was hard for the rich young man when Jesus said he must leave all his wealth aside to follow him; and it is hard for us to accept this today, slaves as we are to a materialistic, greedy culture—too attached to our worldly possessions. Jesus, the Messiah, showed the way into God's kingdom. From the very first moment of the Incarnation, as Saint Paul says, the Word of God emptied himself of his divine attributes and embraced human poverty, taking the form of a servant for our sake.

If Christ had chosen an earthly kingdom, he would have met the expectations of many who surrounded him. Instead, by rejecting worldly possessions and power, he vindicated and validated the poor and lowly of his time, the vulnerable and dispossessed of today. Jesus chose a lifestyle contradictory to that of the world, one of simplicity and poverty, one of total self-emptying. The people of Jesus's time expected a powerful, triumphant Messiah; they knew he would be coming, and they longed for his arrival. Christ knew what was expected of him, what signs the people were looking for, yet he came instead in disguise and challenged them with the truth.

The Lord was meant to be born and to live as a poor man, and to die crucified as a criminal. He challenges us now, as he challenged his disciples, to leave behind preconceived ideas of what the Messiah must be like. If we don't close ourselves to his message, we cannot avoid that he chooses a poor stable as a birthplace and embraces poverty, hardship, sacrifice, and great simplicity as lifestyle. Only by doing like-wise can we understand the mystery of his life, and assimilate the true meaning of his message.

> *What can I give Him,*
> *Poor as I am?*
> *If I were a shepherd,*
> *I would bring a lamb;*
> *If I were a Wise Man,*
> *I would do my part;*
> *Yet what can I give Him:*
> *Give my heart.*
> —from "In the Bleak Midwinter," Christina Rossetti

44.
Christ, the Compassionate Lord

When he saw the crowds, he had compassion for them, because they were harassed and helpless, like sheep without a shepherd.

— Matthew 9:36

Then Jesus called his disciples to him and said, "I have compassion for the crowd, because they have been with me now for three days and have nothing to eat, and I do not want to send them away hungry, for they might faint on the way."

— Matthew 15:32

A leper came to him begging him, and kneeling he said to him, "If you choose, you can make me clean." Moved with pity, Jesus stretched out his hand and touched him, and said to him, "I do choose. Be made clean!"

— Mark 1:40–41

It is impossible to read the Gospels and not be touched by the many stories that show Jesus's infinite compassion for his fellow human beings. The Lord is deeply moved by the sad and often desperate situation of many of his contemporaries.

For instance, in the account related by the Evangelist Mark quoted above, a leper approaches Jesus, saying, "If you choose, you can make me clean." During Jesus's time, lepers were a despised lot, a group of people totally abandoned by society. They were banned from everyday contact with the population and all communal living. Practically speaking, they were just waiting to die. However, on this particular day, the leper intuitively understands that he can trustfully approach Jesus. There is something about the Lord that inspires total confidence; and so, with childlike simplicity, the leper utters his plea. Jesus is moved with compassion. He extends his arm and touches him with his own hand, saying: "I do choose. Be made clean!" As in similar Gospel episodes, we see here how the Lord reacts with a compassion that is uniquely his to the pitiful, painful, distressful human situations he encounters often during his travels throughout Judea.

Always motivated by love and moved with pity, Jesus never hesitates to show his tender compassion to vulnerable and deeply wounded people. Events like this one are repeated again and again throughout the Gospels. Jesus, the God-man, possesses both a unique, divine compassion and a most tender human sensitivity toward each of his fellow human beings, especially the ones he encounters in daily life: lepers, the blind, the poor and deprived, children and widows, the hungry, the sick and the lame, prostitutes and sinners. Jesus feels their pain; he identifies himself with them and then reacts accordingly. He goes out of his way to show empathy and does whatever it takes to improve the present status of these suffering people, eventually bringing consolation and remedy to the situation itself.

When the Word of God became incarnate, he accepted the totality of the human condition except sin. In becoming one of us, Christ embraced wounded humanity with a divine compassion, the type of compassion of which God alone is capable. During his earthly pilgrimage, Jesus showed his compassionate nature and exercised it every time a pressing need arose or someone in pain approached him begging his help. He showed empathy not only for physical needs, illnesses, and the dead, but also—and more importantly—he showed compassion for the spiritual needs of those who surrounded him: he healed souls, he forgave sins, he offered hope to those in despair. Furthermore, he offered consolation and the promise of eternal life to everyone who requested it from him. He lived and demonstrated the compassionate side of his nature to the very end of his life, as in the case of the thief who was nailed to a cross right next to him. When the thief asked Jesus to remember him when he came into his kingdom, Jesus did not judge him. He simply replied, "Today, you will join me in paradise."

Jesus, our compassionate Lord, is a living example of how we his disciples must live and act with compassion toward all. He offers his divine compassion to each and every one of us so that we may in turn offer it to others. We glorify God in our lives when we embrace, willingly and deliberately, the Lord's heartfelt love and his most tender, exquisite, all-embracing compassion. "By this everyone will know that you are my disciples, if you have love for one another" (John 13:35).

Royal Chamber, hail to Thee!
Inn of mercy, house of grace;
Whither weary souls can flee.
Hail to Thee, most loving Heart,
Sorely pierced by sorrow's dart.

Let me enter, let me stay,
Bound by closest ties to Thee;
Graft my heart in Thine, I pray,
That it live no more for me.
This is my ambition's sum,
Heart of Thy Heart to become.
—Angelus Silesius

45.
Christ "Rabboni": Teacher and Master

You call me Teacher and Lord—and you are right, for that is what I am. So if I, your Lord and Teacher, have washed your feet, you also ought to wash one another's feet. For I have set you an example, that you also should do as I have done to you. Very truly, I tell you, servants are not greater than their master.
—John 13:13–16

Now there was a Pharisee named Nicodemus, a leader of the Jews. He came to Jesus by night and said to him, "Rabbi, we know you are a teacher who has come from God; for no one can do these signs that you do apart from the presence of God."
—John 3:1–2

Jesus was praying in a certain place, and after he had finished, one of his disciples said to him, "Lord, teach us to pray, as John taught his disciples."
—Luke 11:1

At age twelve, Jesus left his parents' company and was found teaching the experts in the Temple. From the very beginning of his public life, Christ came to teach his fellow human beings about the kingdom of God. Particularly in his last three years of earthly life, our Lord gave himself to the ministry of teaching and preaching the Good News to his contemporaries, to all who would listen and accept his words. He taught in the local synagogues, in the streets and the marketplaces, in the fields and hills of the Palestinian countryside. He taught at different events and occasions when he was asked or invited. Jesus taught generally in a gentler and more compassionate manner than his cousin, John the Baptist, though always straight to the point. He taught those who surrounded him that God's kingdom was being realized in their midst. He reminded them of the need for repentance and true conversion. He conveyed that God was not only their Creator, but also their Father. As a result of that fatherhood, they all shared in common the same divine life—they were all brothers and sisters in the Lord, and were now called to act as such and to love one another.

As Jesus traveled, he proclaimed continuously that the kingdom of God was at hand. He reminded his listeners that "his hour" was rapidly approaching, and that soon he would be returning to the Father. To those who listened, he offered the gift of faith, and often rewarded those who accepted that faith with miracles. No matter the situation, Jesus never departed from his doctrines or his particular way of teaching and reaching people. His doctrine was the Word of God, which he proclaimed daily and to which he demanded complete allegiance. He proclaimed himself to be the Way, the Truth, and the Life—that there was no other way to reach the Father except through him.

He drew on the Scriptures and the prophets to show his listeners how the ancient prophecies were being fulfilled in him. He taught about the messianic character and purpose of his divine mission. He inspired utter admiration of his knowledge and wisdom. Jesus often taught through the use of parables and symbols of nature, and made recourse to paradoxes and anecdotes. Sometimes he startled an audience with his teachings. Occasionally they were very hard to understand and accept—for example, when he declared himself to be the Son of God, and when he told his disciples that the bread was his body to eat and the wine was his blood to drink.

In the Sermon on the Mount, commonly called "the Beatitudes," Jesus teaches a unique code of moral conduct and says that those who follow it will be recognized as his disciples. And what a code of life and doctrine, indeed! While the world typically exalts the arrogant and the conceited, Jesus promises the kingdom of heaven to the humble and poor in spirit. While the world rewards the powerful and mighty, Jesus conveys a blessing to the meek, and promises them that they will inherit the earth one day. In all societies, past and present, suffering and mourning are counted as evil and something to be avoided. Jesus instead extols them as virtues and promises consolation to those so afflicted. To the hungry and those who thirst for justice, Jesus promises eternal rewards. To those who follow his way of compassion and mercy, he assures that they shall receive mercy themselves one day. To the clean of heart, he promises the vision of God. And to pacifists and peacemakers, an often small crowd in an otherwise violent world, Jesus promises they will be called children of God.

Jesus taught the lessons of the Gospel with the example of his own life. Tragically, few of his contemporaries cared to hear or embrace his teaching fully. He continued to teach them just the same, and made them aware of the truth about eternal life. At all times, he taught with the authority given to him by God the Father, and his teachings always conveyed God's infinite love for his creatures, the very antithesis of all that is evil, egotistic, and selfish in our world. Again and again, Jesus emphasized the reality and truth that God is love, that his one precept is charity, and that those who follow him will be recognized by only one fact: putting the work of love into practice. Thus, Jesus reduced and condensed his teaching to the reality of love in action. For him, love was the climax and sign of true discipleship, the summit of all spiritual living. "God is love, and those who abide in love abide in God, and God abides in them" (1 John 4:16).

> *Lord,*
> *Thou hast given so much to me,*
> *Give one thing more—a grateful heart;*
> *Not thankful when it pleaseth me,*
> *As if thy blessings had spare days;*
> *But such a heart, whose pulse may be*
> *Thy praise.*
> —George Herbert

46.
Christ, Joy of Angels and Delight of Saints

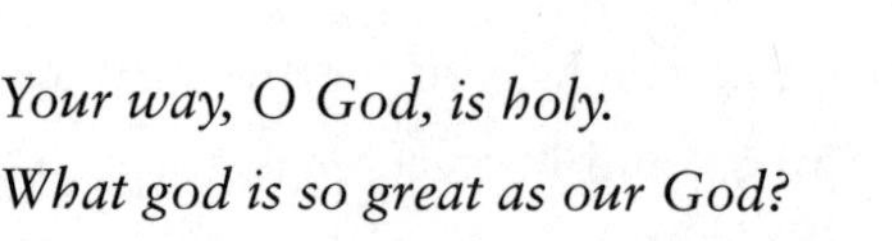

Your way, O God, is holy.
What god is so great as our God?
You are the God who works wonders.
                    —Psalm 77:13–14

Light dawns for the righteous,
and joy for the upright of heart.
Rejoice in the LORD, *O you righteous,*
and give thanks to his holy name.
                    —Psalm 97:11–12

You show me the path of life.
In your presence there is fullness of joy;
in your right hand are pleasures forevermore.
                    —Psalm 16:11

So you have pain now; but I will see you again, and your
hearts will rejoice, and no one will take your joy from
you.

                    —John 16:22

My vision of God is the vision of his love in the communion of saints.
> —Mother Maria, *Her Life in Letters*

In the center apse of our chapel hangs the large icon of the Pantokrator, Christ in majesty, flanked on one side by the Mother of God and on the other by John the Forerunner. The other three wall spaces in our small chapel are filled with icons of the Mother of God, Saint Joseph, the archangels, the apostles, monastic fathers and mothers, and all sorts of saints. They represent God's extended family. They are the *turba magna*, the "vast crowd" mentioned in the book of Revelation. During our liturgical offices, oil lamps and candles burn in front of them in homage and as symbol of our silent prayers. "I believe in the communion of saints," we profess weekly in the Creed. Looking at our chapel, I get a hint of that marvelous communion of saints—and I find it a source of great joy and consolation.

The angels and saints are real, and their presence can be felt. The wonder of it all is that the Theotokos and the saints are also our closest friends, our intercessors. They are there, deep inside the mystery of Christ, to help us, to plead and intercede for us here on earth. We are no longer alone, for through faith we share in the love and joy of God's large extended family.

An essential element of this living communion of saints is its abundant joy, the type of joy that, according to Jesus, "no one can take away from us." Jesus alone is the source and true center of that unique joy. He has obtained our salvation, paid with his own blood to obtain our ransom and redemption. And now we share in the abundant, unequaled joy of God's family.

How marvelous and delightful is the joy the angels and saints share in their eternal home. Face-to-face with the Son of the living God, their souls are enraptured in wonder, love, praise, and endless thanksgiving. As part of that united "vast crowd," they enjoy deep communion inside the mystery of Christ, the mystery of his real presence in their midst. All tears are wiped away, and eternal joy and gladness is theirs forever. "[Lord,] in your presence there is the fullness of joy" (Ps. 16:11).

The presence of the risen Savior, the one source of unspeakable delight to the angels and saints in heaven, is the firm object of our hope on earth. Daily, struggling to manage with our otherwise monotonous tasks and struggles, we live in the blessed hope that one day Jesus will extend to us the invitation: "Enter into the joy of your Lord." Then we too shall know what the angels and saints know and share the fullness of ineffable joy in his presence: the joy of being with Christ and with one another in Christ.

> *There, in your blissful presence, reigns*
> *immortal joy serene;*
> *no wintry storms are heard to roar,*
> *nor desolation seen.*
> *Around you flow unmixed delights,*
> *the rivers deep and wide,*
> *while from the ocean of your love*
> *proceeds an endless tide.*

You of all joy the center are;
oh! never from my soul depart;
Blessed Jesus! Let your saving love,
like dew, drop gently from above.
    —David Addison Harsha

47.
Christ, Power and Wisdom of God

O God of my ancestors and Lord of mercy,
who have made all things by your word,
and by your wisdom have formed humankind
to have dominion over the creatures you have made,
and rule the world in holiness and righteousness,
and pronounce judgment in uprightness of soul,
give me the wisdom that sits by your throne,
and do not reject me from among your servants.
For I am your servant, the son of your serving girl,
a man who is weak and short-lived,
with little understanding of judgment and laws;
for even one who is perfect among human beings
will be regarded as nothing without the wisdom that
comes from you.

—Wisdom 9:1–6

So make up your minds not to prepare your defense in
advance; for I will give you words and a wisdom that
none of your opponents will be able to withstand or
contradict.

—Luke 21:14–15

Saint Paul writes eloquently,

> For the message about the cross is foolishness to those who are perishing, but to us who are being saved it is the power of God. For it is written, 'I will destroy the wisdom of the wise, and the discernment of the discerning I will thwart.' Where is the one who is wise? Where is the scribe? Where is the debater of the age? Has not God made foolish the wisdom of the world? For since, in the wisdom of God, the world did not know God through wisdom, God decided, through the foolishness of our proclamation, to save those who believe (1 Cor. 1:18–21).

In the mystery of the Incarnation, we discover divine wisdom "clothing itself" in our human nature. Later, wisdom reveals itself in Bethlehem, in the weakness of a tiny child. As its revelation continues, wisdom appears to be subjected to obedience, obscurity, and sorrow, appearing at Golgotha, as the suffering servant, the Man of Sorrows. Indeed, as Saint Paul explains, God chooses the foolish things of this world to confound the wise, and the weak things here on earth to confound the strong.

"In the beginning was the Word, and the Word was with God, and the Word was God" (John 1:1). Eternal wisdom is Christ himself, our Savior—long before coming into his own human existence—abiding as the Logos *in sinu Patris*, "in the Father's bosom." This Word devised and created the entire universe, formed all creatures and gave them their proper place, purpose, and mission. He fixed the wonderful order of nature and its seasons. His unique power and wisdom guided and directed all creation. There would be no order in the universe without the power provided by divine wisdom. Jesus, the Word Incarnate, is both the power and the wisdom of God. This wisdom descended from heaven at the moment of the Incarnation, and his power was manifested in the mystery and paradox of the Cross.

O Wisdom, O holy Word of God's mouth,
You govern all creation with your strong yet tender care.
Come and teach us all the ways that lead to life.
　　　　　　　—O Sapientia

Appendices
CHRIST
in Three Distinct
Mystical
Traditions

APPENDIX 1.
Syrian Mystical Tradition:
Early Prayers to Christ

Syrian Christianity is not well known among Christians of the West. This is indeed unfortunate, for the Christian tradition found throughout the Levant goes back to the first oriental Christian communities—which issued directly from the apostles and early Galilean Christians. Small remnants of these Christian communities survive to this day in the Middle East, principally among Syrians, Lebanese, Iraqis, and Palestinians. The liturgical language in some of these communities remains the Aramaic that was spoken by Jesus himself. Unfortunately, in our time, these Christians are fiercely persecuted for their faith, ravaged by local political regimes—caught in the middle of long-standing conflicts, such as those in Palestine and Syria.

While Syrian Christianity has always been influenced by Hellenic culture and the intellectual tendencies of Latin Christianity, it has retained its Semitic-biblical culture, its unique school of thinking, which differentiates it from other types of cultural Christianity. This is evident in Syrian Christianity's profound theological expositions, expressed through the use of poetry and allegory instead of logical argumentation, explaining mystery by making recourse to paradox and rich symbolism rather than analysis and endless definitions as we find in the Scholastic tradition. Saint Ephrem the Syrian and Saint Isaac of Nineveh are among the best-known exponents of this rich, mystical Christian tradition. There are others as well. All of them inherit the amazing Semitic way of explaining the deep mysteries of God that we find in the Scriptures, in particular in the Gospels. The language, expressions, nuances, and symbols are often nearly identical to those articulated by the Lord himself. Christian literature from these Syrian sources thus holds an unbroken continuity with the Gospels.

The following prayers, composed by fathers and monks of this unique Syrian mystical tradition, are but a few from an extensive collection. They are presented here primarily to show that there are other conceptualizations and approaches to the mystery of Christ and, in particular, other very distinct ways of addressing him. Unlike the dualistic view of the world we find in Western and Hellenic cultures, here we feel elated—liberated—to rediscover a rich, positive, unified biblical approach to prayer. The monk Simeon the Graceful, a contemporary of Saint Isaac the Syrian, expressed clearly what this particular way of praying is all about:

Prayer in which the body does not toil by means of the heart, and the heart by means of the mind, together with the intellect and the intelligence, all gathered together in deep-felt groaning, but where instead prayer is just permitted to float across the heart, such prayer, one should realize, is just a miscarriage, for while one is praying, one's mind is drawing away to some other business that one is going to attend to after praying. In such a case one has not yet managed to pray in a unified manner.

Prayers by Saint Isaac of Nineveh[15]

PRAYER 1

As my soul bows to the ground
I offer to you with all my bones
and with all my heart,
the worship that befits you,
O glorious God who dwells in ineffable silence.
You have built for my renewal
a tabernacle of love on earth
where it is your good pleasure to rest,
a temple made of flesh
and fashioned with the most holy sanctuary oil.
Then you filled it with your holy presence
so that worship might be fulfilled in it,
indicating the worship
of the eternal persons of your Trinity
and revealing to the worlds which you had created in your
    grace
an ineffable mystery,
a power which cannot be felt or grasped
by any part of your creation that has come into being.

In wonder at it
angelic beings are submerged in silence,
awed at the dark cloud of this eternal mystery
and at the flood of glory
which issues from within this source of wonder,
for it receives worship
in the sphere of silence
from every intelligence that has been sanctified
and made worthy of you.

PRAYER 2

O Name of Jesus,
key to all gifts,
open up for me the great door of your treasurehouse
so that I may enter and praise you
with the praise that comes from the heart
in return for your mercies
which I have experienced in latter days;
for you came and renewed me
with an awareness of the New World.

I give praise to your holy nature, Lord,
for you have made my nature
a sanctuary for your hiddenness
and a tabernacle for your Mysteries,
a place where you can dwell,
and a holy temple for your divinity.

O Mystery exalted beyond every word
and beyond silence,

who became human in order to renew us

by means of voluntary union with the flesh,

reveal to me the path

by which I may be raised up to your mysteries,

traveling along a course

that is clear and tranquil,

free from the concerns of this world.

Gather my mind into the silence of prayer,

so that all my wandering thoughts

may be silenced within me

during that luminous converse

of supplication and mystery-filled wonder.

PRAYER 3

O Christ who are covered with light

as though with a garment,

who for my sake stood naked in front of Pilate,

clothe me with that might

which you caused to overshadow the saints,

whereby they conquered this world of struggle.

May your divinity, Lord,

take pleasure in me,

and lead me above the world

to be with you.

O Christ, upon whom the many-eyed cherubim

are unable to look

because of the glory of your face

yet out of your love

you received spit upon your face:

remove the shame from my face,

and grant me an open face before you

at the time of prayer.

O Christ, because of our nature's sin

you went out to the wilderness

and vanquished the ruler of darkness,

taking from him the victory

after five thousand years;

force to flee from me him who at all times

forces the human race to sin.

Prayers by Saint Ephrem the Syrian

PRAYER 1

Open up the treasury door for us, Lord,

at the prayers of our supplications;

let our prayers serve as our ambassador,

reconciling us with Your Divinity.

Listen, all who are wise,

pay attention, all who are learned,

acquire understanding and knowledge,

seeing that you are instructed and wise,

I will relate before you the accomplishments of holy prayer.

PRAYER 2

Prayer divided the Red Sea,

allowing the People to cross through its midst;

by the same prayer the sea was reunited once more,

swallowing up Pharoah, the rebellious and impious.
Prayer brought down manna from heaven,
prayer brought down the quails from the sea,
prayer struck the rock in the desert,
causing water to gush forth for the thirsty.

PRAYER 3
Blessed is the person who has consented
to become the close friend of faith
and of prayer:
he lives in singlemindedness
and makes prayer and faith stop by with him.
Prayer that rises up in someone's heart
serves to open up for us the door of heaven:
that person stands in converse with the Divinity
and gives pleasure to the Son of God.
Prayer makes peace with the Lord's anger
and with the vehemence of his wrath.
In this way too, tears that well up in the eyes
can open the door of compassion.

Prayer by John the Elder

O Christ, the ocean of our forgiveness,
allow me to wash off in you
the dirt I am clothed in,
so that I may become resplendent
in the raiment of your holy light.

May I be covered with the cloud of your hidden glory,
full of secret mysteries.
May the things which divert me
from gazing upon your beauty
not be visible to me.
May wonder at your glory
captivate me continually,
may my mind become unable to set in motion
worldly impulses.
May nothing ever separate me from your love,
but rather may that desire,
which is in you,
to behold your countenance
harrow me continually.

Prayers by John of Apamea

PRAYER 1
Praise to you,
without whom everything is empty;
praise to you,
for apart from the praise of you,
all praise is but idle.
Praise to you,
the One who magnifies,
but it is you who are thereby praised,
for you are the object of praise
of everything.

Praise to you,
Perfecter of everything, O Christ.
By your divine teaching you gave wisdom
to all who are instructed by you
to deprive themselves of everything
that belongs to this world
—then they shall be attached to you.
Otherwise, as they traveled after you
while still cleaving to the world,
they might be drawn back by the world into it.
Praise be to you who bade us release ourselves
and then cleave to you,
seeing that, when we are not bound up with anything,
nothing will separate us from you.

PRAYER 2

Praise to you,
O Christ the true Light,
for in you have our souls been illumined
so that we have gained perception
in our minds.
In you we have been made worthy of you,
in you we have found our lives,
and in you we have been acquired by you.
Praise to you,
for in you we have been conjoined to you,
and in you
your glorious Father has taken pleasure in ,
in you we have made peace with him.

You nullified the fierce anger
that Justice had decreed against us,
annulling with your own handwriting
the document which Justice had threateningly inscribed
concerning us.

Praise be to you,
who gave us life in everything.
Thanks be to you, O Lord of all,
for you are true and immutable life,
in whom our treasure will be preserved
and not snatched away:
our wealth will no longer be seized.
Our life is provided for by your care,
and all kinds of wonderful assistance from you
is proffered to us.
It is by these means
that you captivate humanity
to the love of you,
so that all may acquire you
and you may acquire everyone.
Praise to you who proclaimed and taught
that we were to be acquired by you in love.

The Mystical Russian Tradition

The Russian people's concept of Christ evolved slowly from that of the Byzantine Empire, through which they had received the Christian faith. The image of Christ the Pantokrator, based on the role and image of the Byzantine emperor, was gradually replaced with Christ the Savior, recalling Philippians: Christ "emptied himself, taking the form of a servant" (Phil. 2:7 RSV). This is the suffering servant prophesied by Isaiah. The icon of this suffering Christ, also called the Bridegroom, portrays what is sometimes called the *kenosis*, a Greek word meaning "self-emptying." This portrayal was particularly attractive to the Russian people. It conveyed less an idea of authority and instead one of love, forgiveness, meekness, and humiliation, which Christ underwent during his passion.

Devotion to Christ in the Russian tradition is expressed very differently from that in the Western church. It lacks such devotions as the Way of the Cross, Christ the King, and the Sacred Heart. Russians look at Christ, above all, as God and Savior and emphasize the incarnation, passion, and resurrection of the Lord. The Christ we discover in a Russian icon is not sweet or sentimental, as we often see in Western images. On the contrary, he is austere, solemn, and mysterious. His gaze penetrates deeply into our own eyes. He is the Christ who is both Judge and Savior, the Christ who invites us to cling to him alone. This is the Christ who inspired the long akathist prayer included here.

The akathist, a liturgical form of prayer hymn, is a product of the long tradition in the Eastern church. The first one known appears to have been composed in the fifth or sixth century as a hymn of thanksgiving to the Mother of God, the Protectress. It has often been said that the Eastern and Western churches are mutually poor in that they both seem to lack a full and proper understanding of the spiritual tradition that the other possesses. This judgment is clearly indicated in the case of the akathist. Very few Catholics or Protestants have ever heard, let alone prayed, an akathist.

In some respects, these hymns resemble the Western litanies of adoration and supplication, but their particular flavor sets them quite apart. The individual prayers, called kontakions and ikoses, are petitions for temporal protection, wisdom, tranquility of soul, strength of will, and, above all, mercy, which is precisely in keeping with the tenor of Eastern spirituality. They are often framed with a selection from the Gospels, such as Kontakion 2 below: "When You saw the widow weeping by the body of her dead son, O Lord, You were moved to compassion and raised him from the dead. O Lover of mankind, have mercy also upon me, and raise up my sin-tortured soul, that I may sing: Alleluia."

The flavor of these hymns marvelously demonstrates the nature of Eastern spirituality. To understand the akathist is to open oneself to a fuller appreciation of that vast treasury of piety of which we know so little.

The Western lack of appreciation of akathists has been made worse by commentaries of some with only a superficial understanding. One such commentary complains that Eastern Christianity loses man's inherent dignity due to the posture of "abjection" and "timidity before a frightening Deity." On the contrary, the reiterated petition for God's abundant mercy merely recognizes that God's bounty is shown in all things, and that we, his creatures, receive all things from him. Acknowledging that without him we can do nothing, as in the parable of the true vine and its branches, is tremendously inspiring.

The language of these prayers likewise is misunderstood and characterized as flamboyant. God is addressed repeatedly as the "most wonderful," the "most powerful," and so on. This is but a weak rendering of the Slavonic prefix "*pre-*." Actually, the English word "most" can scarcely do these invocations justice; the translation "all-wonderful" is closer, but falls short of the mark as well. Recognizing that the infinite can never be fully grasped by finite minds, the Slavonic prefix is employed to indicate the awesome, staggering import of the beauty and goodness and knowledge that is God. Thus, Christ is referred to as "supreme," "wonderful," and other such terms—so wonderful, in fact, that he is the eternal amazement of the angels. He is called the "infinitely strong," as he would have to be to have achieved what no man has done—namely, to bring himself and all mankind back from the dead. If, then, these rich litanies strike us as being affected, overdone, or excessively emotional, let us try with all our faculties to embrace the intention of the Eastern Christians as they formulated them and as they offer them to God.

This particular akathist is of Russian origin. When Christianity was introduced into Russia from Constantinople in the tenth century, it was natural that the customs and forms of Byzantine liturgical practice come with it. The Russian Christians quickly appropriated the akathist and made it truly their own when they composed this hymn to our Lord—the first, as far as we know, to be addressed specifically to the second person of the Trinity. As we pray the akathist and assimilate the prayerful sentiments and piety it inspires, let us strive to keep in mind an idea of the Christ to whom our prayers are addressed. It makes the praying easier to understand and digest. By entering prayerfully, reverently, into the hymns and praises of the akathist, we begin to discover some of the treasures of Russian spirituality, in particular their deep, deep attachment to the person of Christ.

The Akathist Hymn to Our Lord, the Most Sweet Jesus[16]

PREAMBLE (KONTAKION 1)
Unconquered King and Lord, Vanquisher of the Nether World, I, Your creature and servant, sing Your praise for having delivered me from eternal death. Since Your mercies

are boundless, free me from every harm as I sing: O Jesus, Son of God, have mercy on me!

IKOS 1

Creator of Angels and Lord of Angelic Hosts: as You once opened the ears of the deaf and the mouths of the dumb, empower my dull mind and tongue to sing to You:

O Jesus most wonderful, Marvel of Angels!

O Jesus most powerful, Deliverer of Our Forefathers!

O Jesus most delightful, Exultation of Patriarchs!

O Jesus most glorious, the Might of Rulers!

O Jesus most beloved, the Fulfillment of Prophets!

O Jesus most marvelous, the Strength of Martyrs!

O Jesus most serene, the Joy of Monks!

O Jesus most merciful, the Delight of Priests!

O Jesus most kind, the Happiness of Saints!

O Jesus most honorable, the Chastity of the Chaste!

O Jesus, Everlasting Salvation of Sinners!

O Jesus, Son of God, have mercy on me!

KONTAKION 2

When You saw the widow weeping by the body of her dead son, O Lord, You were moved to compassion and raised him from the dead. O Lover of mankind, have mercy also upon me, and raise up my sin-tortured soul, that I may sing: Alleluia!

IKOS 2

As he sought understanding, Philip, in his confusion said: "Lord, show us the Father." In answer, You told him: "Have I been so long a time with you and you have not known that the Father is in Me and I am in the Father?" Likewise, Incomparable Lord, I cry out with fear:

O Jesus, God Eternal!

O Jesus, Most Powerful King!

O Jesus, Long-suffering Lord!

O Jesus, Ever-merciful Savior!

O Jesus, Ever-gracious Guardian!

O Jesus, cleanse me of sin!

O Jesus, deliver me from all iniquities!

O Jesus, forgive my insincerities!

O Jesus, my Hope, never forsake me!

O Jesus, my Help, do not reject me!

O Jesus, my Creator, do not forget me!

O Jesus, my Shepherd, let me go not astray!

O Jesus, Son of God, have mercy on me!

KONTAKION 3

O Jesus, Who bestowed heavenly power upon the apostles waiting in Jerusalem: fill me, who am deprived of all goodness, with Your Holy Spirit, so that I may lovingly sing to You: Alleluia!

IKOS 3

O Jesus endowed with a richness of compassion, You called the publicans, the unfaithful, and the sinners to You.

Do not despise me, who am like them; but, rather, receive this song as a gift of precious perfume:

O Jesus, Invincible Strength!

O Jesus, Boundless in Mercy!

O Jesus, Unsurpassable in Beauty!

O Jesus, Unspeakable Love!

O Jesus, Son of the Living God!

O Jesus, have mercy on me, a sinner!

O Jesus, listen to me, defiled from birth!

O Jesus, cleanse me, born in sin!

O Jesus, teach me, unworthy though I be!

O Jesus, enlighten my darkness!

O Jesus, cleanse me, a sinner!

O Jesus, restore me, the prodigal!

O Jesus, Son of God, have mercy on me!

KONTAKION 4

With doubts storming within him, Peter began to sink, but looking up, he saw You walking on the water, and, realizing that You are truly God, he accepted the saving hand, exclaiming: Alleluia!

IKOS 4

Hearing You as You passed by, the blind man cried out: "Jesus, Son of David, have mercy on me"; and You, by calling out to him, opened his eyes. Likewise, in Your mercy, open the eyes of my soul, that I may cry out to You:

O Jesus, Creator of the Heavenly Spirits!

O Jesus, Deliverer of the Poor!

O Jesus, Savior from Evil Spirits!

O Jesus, Artist of All Creation!

O Jesus, Comforter of My Soul!

O Jesus, Enlightenment of My Mind!

O Jesus, Joy of My Heart!

O Jesus, Health of My Body!

O Jesus, my Savior, save me!

O Jesus, my Light, enlighten me!

O Jesus, deliver me from all torments!

O Jesus, save me, unworthy though I be!

O Jesus, Son of God, have mercy on me!

KONTAKION 5

Through the shedding of Your Divine Blood, we were freed from the just curse of old. In like manner, free us now from the torments of our evil passions, and from prodigal rebellion and sinful despair with which the serpent defiled us, so that we may sing to You: Alleluia!

IKOS 5

The Jewish children, seeing their Creator incarnate as Man, and recognizing Him as their Lord, hastily cut branches to honor Him, crying out: "Hosanna!" We also offer You this song:

O Jesus, True God!

O Jesus, Son of David!

O Jesus, Most Glorious King!

O Jesus, Innocent Lamb!

O Jesus, Marvelous Shepherd!

O Jesus, Guardian of My Childhood!

O Jesus, Provider of My Youth!

O Jesus, Praise of My Old Age!

O Jesus, My Hope at Death!

O Jesus, My Life after Death!

O Jesus, My Comfort at the Last Judgment!

O Jesus, My Desire, do not cast me off!

O Jesus, Son of God, have mercy on me!

KONTAKION 6

Fulfilling the prophecies and messages of the inspired Prophets, Jesus appeared on earth. Omnipresence lived with men and took upon Himself our weaknesses. And we, being healed by Your wounds, have learned to sing: Alleluia!

IKOS 6

The light of Your truth shines forth throughout the entire universe and destroys the falsehoods of the devil. Idols, being no match for Your power, O Savior, fall down before You. And we, who have received salvation, sing to You:

O Jesus, truly You have destroyed error!

O Jesus, Light Brighter than All Others!

O Jesus, Our King Surpassing All in Strength!

O Jesus, You delight in showing mercy!

O Jesus, Bread of Life, satisfy my hunger!

O Jesus, Fount of Intelligence, quench my thirst for truth!

O Jesus, Garment of Joy, cover me who am
corruptible!

O Jesus, Joyous Shelter, protect me who am unworthy!
O Jesus, Who grants every prayer, grant me tears
   for my sins!
O Jesus, Possession of All Who Seek, possess my soul!
O Jesus, Contemplation of the Wise, open my
   Mind to penance!
O Jesus, Who paid the price for my sinfulness,
   cleanse me of sin!
O Jesus, Son of God, have mercy on me!

KONTAKION 7

Fulfilling the precious mystery revealed from the beginning
of time, You were led as a sheep to the slaughter, and, as
an innocent lamb, You were silent before the shearers.
As God, You rose from the dead, and with glory. You
ascended into heaven, so that we, exalted, might sing to
Him: Alleluia!

IKOS 7

Amazed creation beheld the appearance of the Creator,
Who was born without seed from a Virgin, Who trium-
phantly arose from a sealed grave, and Who physically
came to the apostles through locked doors. And we, being
likewise astonished, now sing:
   O Jesus, Inexplicable Word!
   O Jesus, Incomparable Word!
   O Jesus, Unconquered Strength!
   O Jesus, Indescribable Divinity!

O Jesus, Lord Over All!

O Jesus, Invincible Kingdom!

O Jesus, Unending Sovereignty!

O Jesus, Omnipotent One!

O Jesus, Eternal Power!

O Jesus, My Creator, look graciously upon me!

O Jesus, My Savior, save me!

O Jesus, Son of God, have mercy on me!

KONTAKION 8

Let us cast out the foolishness of the world and turn our minds to the Divine; for the undreamed-of has happened, and God has become man in order to lead us to heaven, so that we might sing to Him: Alleluia!

IKOS 8

You always associated with the lowly. Though incomparably greater than the mighty and wise, You never sought their company. When You willingly suffered for us, You conquered Death by Your death. And by Your resurrection, You gave life to those who sing:

O Jesus, Delight of Our Hearts!

O Jesus, Strength of Our Bodies!

O Jesus, Purity of Our Souls!

O Jesus, Enlightenment of Our Thoughts!

O Jesus, Joy of Our Conscience!

O Jesus, Confident Hope!

O Jesus, Eternal Memory!

O Jesus, the Highest Praise!

O Jesus, Supreme Name!

O Jesus, My Desire, do not cast me away!

O Jesus, My Pastor, look after me!

O Jesus, My Savior, save me!

O Jesus, Son of God, have mercy on me!

KONTAKION 9

O Jesus, all the angelic choirs unceasingly glorify Your most holy Name, singing in the heavens: Holy, Holy, Holy! Likewise, we sinners here on earth sing out with earthly lips: Alleluia!

IKOS 9

O Jesus, Savior, all the ancient prophecies concerning You are feeble. They convey as little as the burbling of fish, for they fail to explain how You remained God and became a perfect man. We, likewise, amazed, sing to You with faith:

O Jesus, Eternally God!

O Jesus, King of Kings!

O Jesus, Judge of the Living and the Dead!

O Jesus, Hope of the Hopeless!

O Jesus, Comforter of Those Who Weep!

O Jesus, Glory of the Lowly!

O Jesus, do not judge me according to my deeds!

O Jesus, let me not despair!

O Jesus, enlighten my spiritual powers!

O Jesus, keep before me the idea of death!

O Jesus, Son of God, have mercy on me!

KONTAKION 10

The Source of Light came to those groping in darkness and, being incarnate, submitted even to death because he wished to save the world. For this reason, Your Name is hymned above all others, and from all heavenly and earthly creation is heard: Alleluia!

IKOS 10

Eternal King, True Comforter, Christ; cleanse us from all sinfulness as You cleansed the ten lepers. Heal us also as You healed the avaricious Zacchaeus, the publican, as we sing to You with love, saying:

O Jesus, Treasury of Immortality!

O Jesus, Abundance of Riches!

O Jesus, Food of the Strong!

O Jesus, Fount Inexhaustible!

O Jesus, Garment of the Poor!

O Jesus, Defender of Widows!

O Jesus, Aid of All Those Who Labor!

O Jesus, Protection of Travelers!

O Jesus, Guide of Seafarers!

O Jesus, Queller of Storms!

O Jesus, raise me up who have fallen!

O Jesus, Son of God, have mercy on me!

KONTAKION 11

Unworthy though it be, we bring to You our most endearing song and sing to You as did the woman of Canaan: "O Jesus, have mercy on me!" We are indeed not Gentiles, but our flesh is stung by the falsehoods of the devil and raging anger. Therefore, heal us who sing: Alleluia!

IKOS 11

A glowing beacon for those who dwell in the darkness of ignorance, Paul persecuted You until he was quelled by the power of Your voice and enlightened quickly by Your heavenly words. In like manner, enlighten the darkened eyes of my soul as I sing:

O Jesus, my King Most Powerful!

O Jesus, my God Most Strong!

O Jesus, my Immortal Master!

O Jesus, my Creator Most Glorious!

O Jesus, my Good Strengthener!

O Jesus, my Most Gentle Pastor!

O Jesus, my Lord Most Compassionate!

O Jesus, my Savior Most Merciful!

O Jesus, banish my dark evil passions!

O Jesus, heal me who am laden with sin!

O Jesus, cleanse me from worldly thoughts!

O Jesus, guard my heart from evil passions!

O Jesus, Son of God, have mercy on me!

KONTAKION 12

O Jesus, Remitter of Debts, grant me the grace to be as repentant as Peter who denied You; and call me, lest I despair, as You earlier called Paul, who persecuted You, and hear me as I sing to You: Alleluia!

IKOS 12

Singing of Your Incarnation, we all praise You and believe like Thomas that, sitting together with the Father, You are Lord and God, and the Judge of the Living and the Dead. Allow me to stand at Your right hand and sing:

> O Jesus, my Eternal King, have mercy on me!
>
> O Jesus, Aroma of Flowers, shed Your Perfume upon me!
>
> O Jesus, Warming Love, enkindle me!
>
> O Jesus, Eternal Temple, shelter me!
>
> O Jesus, Cloak of Light, cover me!
>
> O Jesus, Brilliant Pearl, shine upon me!
>
> O Jesus, Sun of Holiness, illumine me!
>
> O Jesus, Joyful Light, inspire me!
>
> O Jesus, deliver me from all bodily and spiritual ills!
>
> O Jesus, spare me from falling into the hands of evil-doers!
>
> O Jesus, free me from eternal fire and torment!
>
> O Jesus, Son of God, have mercy on me!

KONTAKION 13

O Most Gracious Jesus, Delight of Our Hearts: receive now our humble prayer as You received the two lowly talents of the poor widow. Deliver Your people from every visible and invisible enemy, from foreign invasion, civil war, and riot; from all storms and every distress and illness. Save me from all torment as we sing to You: Alleluia!

IKOS 13

Creator of Angels and Lord of Angelic Hosts: as You once opened the ears of the deaf and the mouths of the mute, empower my dull mind and tongue to sing to You:

O Jesus Most Wonderful, Marvel of Angels!

O Jesus Most Powerful, Deliverer of Our Forefathers!

O Jesus Most Delightful, Exultation of Patriarchs!

O Jesus Most Beloved, the Fulfillment of Prophets!

O Jesus Most Serene, the Joy of Monks!

O Jesus Most Merciful, the Delight of Priests!

O Jesus Most Kind, the Happiness of Saints!

O Jesus Most Honorable, the Chastity of the Chaste!

O Jesus, Everlasting Salvation of Sinners!

O Jesus, Son of God, have mercy on me!

APPENDIX 3.
The Romanian Mystical Tradition: A Witness to the Jesus Prayer

Sweet is the pure and constant remembrance of Jesus abiding in one's heart and the ineffable illumination resulting from it.

—Saint Mark, Bishop of Ephesus

The hesychast tradition of the Jesus Prayer was first introduced in Moldavia. It was carried to many of the monasteries of the Romanian landscape by monks from Mount Athos, where the tradition remains fervent, constant, and alive in our present day. This tradition of prayer has helped Romanian monasteries remain open and functioning, even during the time of persecution.

One of those responsible for the growth the hesychast monastic tradition in Romania was the remarkable Starets Paisius Velichkovsky, abbot and spiritual guide of the monks of the Niametz Monastery in Moldavia. He was a deeply gifted leader, who combined the three necessary elements—holiness, love of learning, and a talent for organizing community life—to an astonishing degree. His personal holiness attracted many new disciples who later expanded his work throughout Romania, the Ukraine, and even Russia. Starets Paisius stressed the necessity of working continually on translations of both patristic and ancient monastic literature, on the correction of existing texts, and on the production of new spiritual literature to guide future monks and spiritual seekers.

The influence of these translations, new literature, and improved texts that Starets Paisius initiated and encouraged was immense. It affected not only monastics in Romania, Russia, and Serbia, but also people of all classes and backgrounds. The Niametz Monastery became a true spiritual center of renewal, particularly through its emphasis of the assiduous, continual practice of the Jesus Prayer. Through the Jesus Prayer, Starets Paisius counseled, the monk is able to participate in God's holiness and spiritual action, and is also able to unite his mind with God through inexpressible love. He often quoted the words of Saint Symeon of Thessalonica:

This divine prayer of our Savior consists of this appeal: Lord Jesus Christ, Son of God, have mercy on me. This prayer is supplication, confession of faith, the giver of the Holy Spirit and the bestower of divine gifts, the purification of the heart, the expulsion of demons, the indwelling of Jesus Christ, the source of spiritual ideas and divine thoughts, deliverance from sins, the ministering to souls and bodies, the giver of divine illumination and the source of God's mercy, the giver of revelations and divine mysteries to the meek, and it is salvation itself, for it carries within itself the saving name of our God—this being the name of Jesus Christ the Son of God which was betrothed to us.

Many years later, one beneficiary of the spiritual work of the starets and his disciples was Mother Alexandra of Romania. Born Princess Ileana of Romania in 1909, she was the youngest daughter of King Ferdinand and Queen Marie. In 1931 she married Archduke Anton of Austria. They had six children. Forced out of Eastern Europe by the Communist government in 1948, the family resettled in Newton, Massachusetts. She divorced the Archduke in 1954, remarried, and divorced again. With her children grown, she entered the Monastery of the Protection of the Holy Mother of God in France in 1961, then returned to America six years later to found the Orthodox Monastery of the Transfiguration in Ellwood City, Pennsylvania.

In the exposition which follows, written in the 1950s, Mother Alexandra relates the story of her own encounter with the tradition of the Jesus Prayer in her native country, and the permanent impact it had on her for the rest of her life:

I have often read the Jesus Prayer in prayer books and heard it in church, but my attention was drawn to it first some years ago in Romania. There in a small Monastery of Sâmbata, tucked away at the foot of the Carpathians in the heart of the deep forest, its little white church reflected in a crystal-clear mountain pond, I met a monk who practiced the "prayer of the heart." Profound peace and silence reigned at Sâmbata in those days; it was a place of rest and strength—I pray God it still is.

I have wandered far since I last saw Sâmbata, and all the while the Jesus Prayer lay as a precious gift buried in my heart. It remained inactive until a few years ago, when I read *The Way of a Pilgrim*. Since then I have been seeking to practice it continually. At times I lapse; nonetheless, the prayer has opened unbelievable vistas within my heart and soul.

The Jesus Prayer, or the Prayer of the Heart, centers on the Holy Name itself. It may be said in its entirety: "Lord Jesus Christ, Son of God, have mercy upon me, a sinner"; it may be changed to "us sinners" or to other persons named, or it may be shortened. The power lies in the name of Jesus; thus "Jesus," alone, may fulfill the whole need of the one who prays.

The Prayer goes back to the New Testament and has had a long, traditional use. The method of contemplation based upon the Holy Name is attributed to St. Simeon, called the "New Theologian" (949–1022). When he was 14 years old, St. Simeon had a vision of heavenly light in which he seemed to be separated from his body. Amazed, and overcome with an overpowering joy, he felt a consuming humility, and cried, borrowing the Publican's prayer (Luke 18:13), "Lord Jesus, have mercy upon me." Long after the vision had disappeared, the great joy returned to St. Simeon each time he repeated the prayer; and he taught his disciples to worship likewise. The prayer evolved into its expanded form: "Lord Jesus Christ, Son of God, have mercy upon me, a sinner." In this guise it has come down to us from generation to generation of pious monks and laymen.

The invocation of the Holy Name is not peculiar to the Orthodox Church but is used by Roman Catholics, Anglicans, and Protestants, though to a lesser degree. On Mount Sinai and Athos the monks worked out a whole system of contemplation based upon this simple prayer, practiced in complete silence. These monks came to be known as "Quietists" (in Greek: "Hesychasts").

St. Gregory Palamas (1296–1359), the last of the great Church Fathers, became *the* exponent of the Hesychasts. He won, after a long drawn out battle, an irrefutable place for the Jesus Prayer and the Quietists within the Church. In the 18th century when tsardom hampered monasticism in Russia, and the Turks crushed Orthodoxy in Greece, the Neamtzu monastery in Moldavia (Romania) became one of the great centers for the Jesus Prayer.

The Prayer is held to be so outstandingly spiritual because it is focused wholly on Jesus: all thoughts, striving, hope, faith and love are outpoured in devotion to God the Son. It fulfills two basic injunctions of the New Testament. In one, Jesus said: "I say unto you, Whatsoever ye shall ask the Father in my name, he will give it you. Hitherto have ye asked nothing in my name: ask, and ye shall receive, that your joy may be full" (John 16:23, 24). In the other precept we find St. Paul's injunction to pray without ceasing (1 Thess. 5:17). Further, it follows Jesus's instructions upon how to pray (which he gave at the same time he taught his followers the Lord's Prayer): "When thou prayest, enter into thy closet, and when thou hast shut thy door, pray to thy Father which is in secret; and thy Father which seeth in secret shall reward thee openly" (Matt. 6:6).

And Jesus taught that all impetus, good and bad, originates in men's hearts. "A good man out of the good treasure of his heart bringeth forth that which is good; and an evil man out of the evil treasure of his heart bringeth forth that which is evil: for of the abundance of the heart his mouth speaketh" (Luke 6:45).

Upon these and many other precepts of the New Testament as well as the Old, the Holy Fathers, even before St. Simeon, based their fervent and simple prayer. They developed a method of contemplation in which unceasing prayer became as natural as breathing, following the rhythmic cadence of the heart beat.

All roads that lead to God are beset with pitfalls because the enemy (Satan) ever lies in wait to trip us up. He naturally attacks most assiduously when we are bent on finding our way to salvation, for that is what he most strives to hinder. In mystical prayer the temptations we encounter exceed all others in danger; because our thoughts are on a higher level, the allurements are proportionally subtler. Someone said that "mysticism started in mist and ended in schism"; this cynical remark, spoken by an unbeliever, has a certain truth in it. Mysticism is of real spiritual value only when it is practiced with absolute sobriety.

At one time a controversy arose concerning certain Quietists who fell into excessive acts of piety and fasting because they lost the sense of moderation upon which our Church lays so great a value. We need not dwell upon misuses of the Jesus Prayer, except to realize that all exaggerations are harmful and that we should at all times use self-restraint. "Practice of the Jesus Prayer is the traditional fulfillment of the injunction of the Apostle Paul to 'pray always': it has nothing to do with the mysticism which is the heritage of pagan ancestry" (Foreword of *Writings from the Philokalia*).

The Orthodox Church is full of deep mystic life which she guards and encompasses with the strength of her traditional rules; thus her mystics seldom go astray. "The 'ascetical life' is a life in which 'acquired' virtues, i.e., virtues resulting from a personal effort, only accompanied by that general grace which God grants to every good will, prevail. The 'mystical life' is a life in which the gifts of the Holy Spirit are predominant over human efforts, and in which 'infused' virtues are predominant over the 'acquired' ones; the soul has become more passive than active. Let us use a classical comparison. Between the ascetic life, that is, the life in which human action predominates, and the mystical life, that is, the life in which God's action predominates, there is the same difference as between rowing a boat and sailing it; the oar is the ascetic effort, the sail is the mystical passivity which is unfurled to catch the divine wind" (*Orthodox Spirituality*, A Monk of the Eastern Church). The Jesus Prayer is the core of mystical prayer, and it can be used by anyone, at any time. There is nothing mysterious about this (let us not confuse "mysterious" with "mystic"). We start by following the precepts and examples frequently given by our Lord. First, go aside into a quiet place: "Come ye yourselves apart into a desert place, and rest awhile" (Mark 6:31); "Study to be quiet" (1 Thess. 4:11); then pray in secret—alone and in silence.

The phrases "to pray in secret alone and in silence" need, I feel, a little expanding. "Secret" should be understood as it is used in the Bible: for instance, Jesus tells us to do our charity secretly—not letting the left hand know what the right one does. We should not parade our devotions, nor boast about them. "Alone" means to separate ourselves from our immediate surroundings and disturbing influences. As a matter of fact, never are we in so much company as when we pray ". . . seeing we also are compassed about with so great a cloud of witnesses . . ." (Hebrews 12:1). The witnesses are all those who pray: Angels, Archangels, saints and sinners, the living and the dead. It is in prayer, especially the Jesus Prayer, that we become keenly aware of belonging to the living body of Christ. In "silence" implies that we do not speak our prayer audibly. We do not even meditate on the words; we use them only to reach beyond them to the essence itself.

In our busy lives this is not easy, yet it can be done—we can each of us find a few minutes in which to use a prayer consisting of only a few words, or even only one. This prayer should be repeated quietly, unhurriedly, thoughtfully. Each thought should be concentrated on Jesus, forgetting all else, both joys and sorrows. Any stray thought, however good or pious, can become an obstacle.

When you embrace a dear one you do not stop to meditate how and why you love—you just love whole-heartedly. It is the same when spiritually we grasp Jesus the Christ to our heart. If we pay heed to the depth and quality of our love, it means that we are preoccupied with our own reactions, rather than giving ourselves unreservedly to Jesus—holding nothing back. *Think* the prayer as you breathe in and out; calm both mind and body, using as rhythm the heartbeat. Do not search for words, but go on repeating the Prayer, or Jesus's name alone, in love and adoration. That is ALL! Strange—in this little there is more than all!

It is good to have regular hours for prayer and to retire whenever possible to the same room or place, possibly before an icon. The icon is loaded with the objective presence of the One depicted, and thus greatly assists our invocation. Orthodox monks and nuns find that to use a rosary helps to keep the attention fixed. Or you may find it best quietly to close your eyes—focusing them inward.

The Jesus Prayer can be used for worship and petition; as intercession, invocation, adoration, and as thanksgiving. It is a means by which we lay all that is in our hearts, both for God and man, at the feet of Jesus. It is a means of communion with God and with all those who pray. The fact that we can train our hearts to go on praying even when we sleep, keeps us uninterruptedly within the community of prayer. This is no fanciful statement; many have experienced this life-giving fact. We cannot, of course, attain this continuity of prayer all at once, but it is achievable; for all that is worthwhile we must ". . . run with patience the race that is set before us . . ." (Hebrews 12:1).

I had a most striking proof of uninterrupted communion with all those who pray when I lately underwent surgery. I lay long under anesthesia. "Jesus" had been my last conscious thought, and the first word on my lips as I awoke. It was marvelous beyond words to find that although I knew nothing of what was happening to my body I never lost cognizance of being prayed-for and of praying myself. After such an experience one no longer wonders that there are great souls who devote their lives exclusively to prayer.

Prayer has always been of very real importance to me, and the habit formed in early childhood of morning and evening prayer has never left me; but in the practice of the Jesus Prayer I am but a beginner. I would, nonetheless, like to awaken interest in this prayer because, even if I have only touched the hem of a heavenly garment, I have touched it—and the joy is so great I would share it with others. It is not every man's way of prayer; you may not find in it the same joy that I find, for your way may be quite a different one—yet equally bountiful.

In fear and joy, in loneliness and companionship, it is ever with me. Not only in the silence of daily devotions, but at all times and in all places. It transforms, for me, frowns into smiles; it beautifies, as if a film had been washed off an old picture so that the colors appear clear and bright, like nature on a warm spring day after a shower. Even despair has become attenuated and repentance has achieved its purpose.

When I arise in the morning, it starts me joyfully upon a new day. When I travel by air, land, or sea, it sings within my breast. When I stand upon a platform and face my listeners, it beats encouragement. When I gather my children around me, it murmurs a blessing. And at the end of a weary day, when I lay me down to rest, I give my heart over to Jesus: "(Lord) into thy hands I commend my spirit." I sleep—but my heart as it beats prays on: "JESUS."[17]

Notes

EPIGRAPH

1   "His mercy for us is strong; the faithfulness of the LORD is forever" (Ps. 117:2 NABRE).

1. WE CONFESS CHRIST, OUR GOD

2   Saint Cyril (Patriarch of Alexandria), *Against Those Who Are Unwilling to Confess that the Holy Virgin Is Theotokos*, trans. George Dion. Dragas (Rollinsford, NH: Orthodox Research Institute, 2004), 13.

10. CHRIST, SON OF THE LIVING GOD

3   Ibid.

16. JESUS OF NAZARETH

4   Charles de Foucauld, *Meditations of a Hermit* (London: Oates & Washbourne, 1930).

18. CHRIST'S BANQUET HALL: LIVING MANNA AND BREAD FROM HEAVEN

5   Matthew the Poor, *The Titles of Christ* (Rollinsford, NH: Orthodox Research Institute, 2008).

19. JESUS AT MT. TABOR:
THE TRANSFIGURED LORD

6   Sticheras are hymns sung in the Byzantine Rite during the morning and evening services.

30. CHRIST THE MERCIFUL

7   Olga Poloukhine, iconographer and artist; website: http://studio.poloukhine.com.

32. CHRIST THE GIVER OF LIFE

8   Alexander Schmemann, *For the Life of the World: Sacraments and Orthodoxy* (Crestwood, NY: St. Vladimir's Seminary Press, 1973).

34. FOLLOWING CHRIST: THE PURPOSE
OF THE MONASTIC LIFE

9   Thomas Merton, *The Monastic Journey*, ed. Patrick Hart, ocso (Kalamazoo, MI: Cistercian Publications, 1992).

10   Saint Benedict, *The Holy Rule of Our Most Holy Father Benedict*, trans. Rev. Boniface F. Verheyen, osb (Atchison, KS: Abbey Student Press, St. Benedict's College, 1949), ch. 71.

35. THE JESUS PRAYER

11   Archimandrite Sophrony, *On Prayer*, trans. Rosemary Edmonds (Crestwood, NY: St. Vladimir's Seminary Press, 1998).

36. A CHRIST-CENTERED LIFE:
SAINT BENEDICT

12   Saint Benedict, *The Holy Rule of Our Most Holy Father Benedict*, trans. Rev. Boniface F. Verheyen, osb (Atchison, KS: Abbey Student Press, St. Benedict's College, 1949), ch. 4.

13 Thomas Merton, *The Silent Life* (New York: Farrar, Straus & Cudahy, 1957), xi.

38. THE MONK'S ATTACHMENT TO CHRIST

14 Saint Benedict, *The Holy Rule of Our Most Holy Father Benedict*, trans. Rev. Boniface F. Verheyen, OSB (Atchison, KS: Abbey Student Press, St. Benedict's College, 1949), prologue.

APPENDIX 1.
SYRIAN MYSTICAL TRADITION:
EARLY PRAYERS TO CHRIST

15 All prayers in Appendix 1, "Syrian Mystical Tradition," taken from *The Syriac Fathers on Prayer and the Spiritual Life*, introduced and translated by Sebastian Brock. Copyright 1987 by Cistercian Publications, Inc. © 2008 by the Order of Saint Benedict, Collegeville, Minnesota. Used with permission.

APPENDIX 2.
THE MYSTICAL RUSSIAN TRADITION

16 Adapted from a public domain version in *Byzantine Catholic Prayer for the Home*, obtained at Internet Archive, accessed August 1, 2016, https://archive.org/details/ByzantineCatholicPrayerForTheHome, 16.

APPENDIX 3.
THE ROMANIAN MYSTICAL
TRADITION: A WITNESS TO THE JESUS PRAYER

17 H.R.H. Princess Ileana of Romania, *Introduction to the Jesus Prayer* (Cincinnati, OH: Forward Movement Publications, 1959). Used with permission of the publisher.

ABOUT PARACLETE PRESS

WHO WE ARE

Paraclete Press is a publisher of books, recordings, and DVDs on Christian spirituality. Our publishing represents a full expression of Christian belief and practice—from Catholic to Evangelical, from Protestant to Orthodox.

We are the publishing arm of the Community of Jesus, an ecumenical monastic community in the Benedictine tradition. As such, we are uniquely positioned in the marketplace without connection to a large corporation and with informal relationships to many branches and denominations of faith.

WHAT WE ARE DOING

PARACLETE PRESS BOOKS | Paraclete publishes books that show the richness and depth of what it means to be Christian. Although Benedictine spirituality is at the heart of all that we do, we publish books that reflect the Christian experience across many cultures, time periods, and houses of worship. We publish books that nourish the vibrant life of the church and its people.

We have several different series, including the best-selling Paraclete Essentials and Paraclete Giants series of classic texts in contemporary English; Voices from the Monastery—men and women monastics writing about living a spiritual life today; award-winning poetry; best-selling gift books for children on the occasions of baptism and first communion; and the Active Prayer Series that brings creativity and liveliness to any life of prayer.

MOUNT TABOR BOOKS | Paraclete's newest series, Mount Tabor Books, focuses on the arts and literature as well as liturgical worship and spirituality, and was created in conjunction with the Mount Tabor Ecumenical Centre for Art and Spirituality in Barga, Italy.

PARACLETE RECORDINGS | From Gregorian chant to contemporary American choral works, our recordings celebrate the best of sacred choral music composed through the centuries that create a space for heaven and earth to intersect. Paraclete Recordings is the record label representing the internationally acclaimed choir Gloriæ Dei Cantores, praised for their "rapt and fathomless spiritual intensity" by *American Record Guide*; the Gloriæ Dei Cantores Schola, specializing in the study and performance of Gregorian chant; and the other instrumental artists of the Gloriæ Dei Artes Foundation.

Paraclete Press is also privileged to be the exclusive North American distributor of the recordings of the Monastic Choir of St. Peter's Abbey in Solesmes, France, long considered to be a leading authority on Gregorian chant.

PARACLETE VIDEO | Our DVDs offer spiritual help, healing, and biblical guidance for a broad range of life issues including grief and loss, marriage, forgiveness, facing death, bullying, addictions, Alzheimer's, and spiritual formation.

Learn more about us at our website:
www.paracletepress.com or phone us
toll-free at 1.800.451.5006

SCAN
TO
READ
MORE